Science in Our World

Volume Three

Coordinates with National Science Education Standards

creating a window
cleaner company

Dirt Alert—
The Chemistry of Cleaning

why should we
sanitize and disinfect?

preparing and
testing lard soap

making a liquid
hand soap

Diversey

Developed with funding from the National Science Foundation
and Diversey Corporation, Cincinnati, Ohio

Dirt Alert—
The Chemistry of Cleaning

Developed in collaboration with

Diversey Corporation
(now JohnsonDiversey)

Series Editor
Mickey Sarquis, Director
Center for Chemistry Education

This project was supported, in part, by the National Science Foundation. Any opinions, findings, and conclusions or recommendations expressed in this material are those of the authors and do not necessarily reflect the views of the National Science Foundation. The Government has certain rights to this material. This material is based upon work supported by the National Science Foundation under Grant No. TPE-9153930.

Center for
Chemistry Education

This monograph is intended for use by teachers, chemists, and properly supervised students. Teachers and other users must develop and follow procedures for the safe handling, use, and disposal of chemicals in accordance with local and state regulations and requirements. The cautions, warnings, and safety reminders associated with the doing of experiments and activities involving the use of chemicals and equipment contained in this publication have been compiled from sources believed to be reliable and to represent the best opinion on the subject as of 1995. However, no warranty, guarantee, or representation is made by the editor, contributors, Diversey Corporation, or the Terrific Science Press™ as to the correctness or sufficiency of any information herein. Neither the editor, contributors, Diversey Corporation, or the Terrific Science Press assumes any responsibility or liability for the use of the information herein, nor can it be assumed that all necessary warnings and precautionary measures are contained in this publication. Other or additional information or measures may be required or desirable because of particular or exceptional conditions or circumstances, or because of new or changed legislation.

Contributors

Industrial Mentors

Carole Marquardt*
Chemist II, Diversey Corporation
Cincinnati, Ohio

Jeff Little*
Manager of Manufacturing Industries, Diversey Corporation
Cincinnati, Ohio

Linda Coffey*
Manager of Facilities Maintenance, Manager of Nonprocess Chemicals,
and Manager for New Raw Materials, Diversey Corporation
Cincinnati, Ohio

Academic Mentor

Jim Hershberger
Professor, Department of Chemistry, Miami University
Oxford, Ohio

Peer Mentor

Rex Bucheit
Principal, Fillmore Elementary School
Hamilton, Ohio

* Photo not available.

Principal Investigators

Mickey Sarquis — Miami University, Middletown, Ohio
Jim Coats — Dow Chemical USA (retired), Findlay, Ohio
Dan McLoughlin — Xavier University, Cincinnati, Ohio
Rex Bucheit — Fillmore Elementary School, Hamilton, Ohio

Partners for Terrific Science Advisory Board

Table of Contents

Acknowledgments

The authors and editor wish to thank the following individuals who have contributed to the development of the *Science in Our World* series of Teacher Resource Modules.

Terrific Science Press Design and Production Team
Susan Gertz, Amy Stander, Lisa Taylor, Thomas Nackid, Stephen Gentle, Vickie Fultz, Anne Munson, Amy Hudepohl, Andrea Nolan, Pamela Mason

Reviewers

Susan Hershberger	Miami University, Oxford, Ohio
Baird Lloyd	Miami University, Middletown, Ohio
Diane Rose	Ursuline Academy, Cincinnati, Ohio
Mark Sabo	Miami University, Middletown, Ohio
Dave Tomlin	Wright Patterson Air Force Base, Dayton, Ohio
Linda Woodward	University of Southwestern Louisiana, Lafayette, Louisiana

Foreword

Dirt Alert—The Chemistry of Cleaning is one of the *Science in Our World* Teacher Resource Modules. This set is aimed at enabling teachers to introduce their students to the concepts and processes of industrial chemistry and relate these concepts to the consumer products students encounter daily. These hands-on, problem-solving activities help connect science lessons with real life.

Developed as a collaborative effort between industrial, academic, and teacher peer mentors in the *Partners for Terrific Science* program, this module provides background information on the institutional products industry and Diversey's role in this industry, as well as a content review of institutional products chemistry and pedagogical strategies. The activities in this module have been tested by participants in *Partners* programs and by *Partners* teachers in their classrooms, and reviewed by experts in the field to help ensure accuracy, safety, and pedagogical effectiveness.

Partners for Terrific Science, established in 1986, is an industrial/academic partnership that facilitates interaction among classroom teachers, industrial scientists and engineers, and university chemistry faculty to make science education more interesting, relevant, and understandable for all students. The partnership is supported by the Ohio Chemical Council and its more than 100 members, the National Science Foundation, the U.S. Department of Education, the Ohio Board of Regents, the American Chemical Society—Cincinnati Section, Miami University, and over 50 private-sector partners. Diversey Corporation has collaborated in the development of this module.

The Teacher Resource Modules have been developed especially for teachers who want to use industry-based physical science activities in the classroom, but who may not have been able to attend a *Partners* workshop at the Miami site or one of the Affiliate sites nationwide. We want to thank all the contributors, participants, and mentors who made this publication possible.

We hope you will find that these Teacher Resource Modules provide you with a useful and exciting way to involve your students in doing chemistry through integrated real-world themes. We welcome your comments at any time and are interested in learning about especially successful uses of these materials.

Mickey Sarquis, Director
Center for Chemistry Education
July 1995

Partnership Network

We appreciate the dedication and contributions of the following corporations and organizations, who together make *Partners for Terrific Science* a true partnership for the betterment of chemical education for all teachers and students.

Partners in the Private Sector

A & B Foundry, Inc.
Aeronca, Inc.
Ag Renu
Air Products and Chemicals, Inc.
Armco, Inc.
Armco Research and Technology
ARW Polywood
Ashland Chemical Company
Bank One
BASF
Bay West Paper Corporation
Black Clawson Company
BP America: BP Oil, BP Chemicals
Coats & Clark
Crystal Tissue Company
DataChem Laboratories, Inc.
Diversey Corporation
Ronald T. Dodge Company
Dover Chemical Corporation
EG&G Mound Applied Technologies
Fluor Daniel Fernald, Inc.
Formica
Golden Pond Resources

Henkel Corporation, Emery Group
Hewlett-Packard Company
Hilton Davis Company
Hoechst Marion Roussel, Inc.
Inland Container Corporation
Jefferson Smurfit Corporation
JLJ, Inc.
Magnode Corporation
Middletown Paperboard Corporation
Middletown Regional Hospital
Middletown Wastewater Treatment Plant
Middletown Water Treatment Plant
Miller Brewing Company
The Monsanto Fund
Owens Corning Science & Technology Laboratories
The Procter & Gamble Company
Quality Chemicals
Quantum Chemical Corporation
Rumpke Waste Removal/Recycling
Shepherd Chemical Company
Shepherd Color Company
Square D Company
Sun Chemical Corporation

Partners in the Public Sector

Hamilton County Board of Education
Indiana Tech-Prep
Miami University
Middletown Clean Community
National Institute of Environmental Health Sciences
National Science Foundation
Ohio Board of Regents

Ohio Department of Education
Ohio Environmental Protection Agency
Ohio Tech-Prep
State Board for Technical and Comprehensive Education, Columbia, SC
US Department of Education
US Department of Energy, Cincinnati, OH

Professional Societies

American Association of Physics Teachers
African American Math-Science Coalition
American Chemical Society— Central Regional Council
American Chemical Society— Cincinnati Section
American Chemical Society— Dayton Section
American Chemical Society—POLYED
American Chemical Society— Technician Division
American Chemical Society, Washington, DC

American Institute of Chemical Engineers
Chemical Manufacturers Association
Chemistry Teachers Club of New York
Intersocietal Polymer and Plastics Education Initiative
Minorities in Mathematics, Science and Engineering
National Organization of Black Chemists and Chemical Engineers—Cincinnati Section
National Science Teachers Association
Ohio Chemical Council
Science Education Council of Ohio
Society of Plastics Engineers

More than 3,000 teachers are involved in and actively benefiting from this Network.

An Invitation to Industrial Chemists

It is not unusual to hear children say they want to be doctors, astronauts, or teachers when they grow up. It is easy for children to see adults they admire doing these jobs in books, on television, and in real life. But where are our aspiring chemists? The chemist portrayed on television often bears close resemblance to Mr. Hyde: an unrealistic and unfortunate role model.

Children delight in learning and enjoy using words like "stegosaurus" and "pterodactyl." Wouldn't it be wonderful to hear words like "chromatography" and "density" used with the same excitement? You could be introducing elementary school students to these words for the first time. And imagine a 10-year-old child coming home from school and announcing, "When I grow up, I want to be a chemist!" You can be the one responsible for such enthusiasm. By taking the time to visit and interact with an elementary or middle school classroom as a guest scientist, you can become the chemist who makes the difference.

You are probably aware that many non-chemists, including many prehigh school teachers, find science in general (and chemistry in particular) mysterious and threatening. When given a chance, both teachers and students can enjoy transforming the classroom into a laboratory and exploring like real scientists. Consider being the catalyst for this transformation.

Unlike magicians, scientists attempt to find explanations for why and how things happen. Challenge students to join in on the fun of searching for explanations. At the introductory level, it is far more important to provide nonthreatening opportunities for the students to postulate "why?" than it is for their responses to be absolutely complete. If the accepted explanation is too complex to discuss, maybe the emphasis of the presentation is wrong. For example, discussions focusing on the fact that a color change can be an indication of a chemical reaction may be more useful than a detailed explanation of the reaction mechanisms involved.

Because science involves the process of discovery, it is equally important to let the students know that not all the answers are known and that they too can make a difference. Teachers should be made to feel that responses like "I don't know. What do you think?" or "Let's find out together," are acceptable. It is also important to point out that not everyone's results will be the same. Reinforce the idea that a student's results are not wrong just because they are different from a classmate's results.

While using the term "chemistry," try relating the topics to real-life experiences and integrating topics into non-science areas. After all, chemistry is all around us, not just in the chemistry lab.

When interacting with students, take care to involve all of them. It is very worthwhile to spend time talking informally with small groups or individual students before, during, or after your presentation. It is important to convey the message that chemistry is for all who are willing to apply themselves to the questions before them. Chemistry is neither sexist, racist, nor frightening.

For more information on becoming involved in the classroom and a practical and valuable discussion of some do's and don'ts, a resource is available. The American Chemical Society Education Division has a video called *Chemists in the Classroom*. You may purchase this video from American Chemical Society, Washington, DC; 800/227-5558; *http://store.acs.org/cgi-bin/acsonline.storefront/*.

How to Use This Teacher Resource Module

This section is an introduction to the Teacher Resource Module and its organization. The industry featured in this module is the institutional products industry.

How Is This Resource Module Organized?

The Teacher Resource Module is organized into the following main sections: How to Use This Teacher Resource Module (this section), Background for Teachers, Using the Activities in the Classroom, and Activities and Demonstrations. The Background for Teachers section includes Overview of the Institutional Products Industry, Overview of Diversey Corporation, and Content Review. Using the Activities in the Classroom includes Pedagogical Strategies, an Annotated List of Activities and Demonstrations, and a Curriculum Placement Guide. The following paragraphs provide a brief overview of the *Dirt Alert—The Chemistry of Cleaning* module.

Background for Teachers

Overviews of the institutional products industry and Diversey Corporation's role in the industry provide information on the industrial aspect of these activities. The Content Review section is intended to provide you, the teacher, with an introduction to (or a review of) the concepts covered in the module. The material in this section (and in the individual activity explanations) intentionally gives you information at a level beyond what you will present to your students. You can then evaluate how to adjust the content presentation for your own students.

The Content Review section in this module covers the following topics:
- A Review of Mixtures and Compounds
- Formulating Mixtures and Synthesizing Compounds
- Solving Some Industrial Cleaning Problems

Using the Activities in the Classroom

The Pedagogical Strategies section provides ideas for effectively teaching a unit on the institutional products industry. It suggests a variety of ways to incorporate the industry-based activities presented in the module into your curriculum. The Annotated List of Activities and Demonstrations and the Curriculum Placement Guide provide recommended grade levels, descriptions of the activities, and recommended placement of the activities within a typical curriculum.

Module Activities

Each module activity provides complete instructions for conducting the activity in your classroom. These activities have been classroom-tested by teachers like yourself and have been demonstrated to be practical, safe, and effective in the typical classroom. The following information is provided for each activity:

Recommended Grade Level:	The grade levels at which the activity will be most effective are listed.
Group Size:	The optimal student group size is listed.
Time for Preparation:	This includes time to set up for the activity before beginning with the students.

Time for Procedure:	An estimated time for conducting the activity is listed. This time estimate is based on feedback from classroom testing, but your time may vary depending on your classroom and teaching style.
Materials:	Materials are listed for each part of the activity, divided into amounts per class, per group, and per student.
Resources:	Sources for difficult-to-find materials are listed.
Safety and Disposal:	Special safety and/or disposal procedures are listed if required.
Getting Ready:	Information is provided in Getting Ready when preparation is needed prior to beginning the activity with the students.
Opening Strategy:	A strategy for introducing the topic to be covered and for gaining the students' interest is suggested.
Procedure:	The steps in the Procedure are directed toward you, the teacher, and include cautions and suggestions where appropriate.
Variations and Extensions:	Variations are alternative methods for doing the Procedure. Extensions are methods for furthering student understanding.
Discussion:	Possible questions for students are provided.
Explanation:	The Explanation is written to you, the teacher, and is intended to be modified for students.
Key Science Concepts:	Targeted key science topics are listed.
Cross-Curricular Integration:	Cross-Curricular Integration provides suggestions for integrating the science activity with other areas of the curriculum.
References:	References used to write this activity are listed.

Notes and safety cautions are included in activities as needed and are indicated by the following icons and type style:

 Notes are preceded by an arrow.

 Cautions are preceded by an exclamation point.

Employing Appropriate Safety Procedures

Experiments, demonstrations, and hands-on activities add relevance, fun, and excitement to science education at any level. However, even the simplest activity can become dangerous when the proper safety precautions are ignored or when the activity is done incorrectly or performed by students without proper supervision. While the activities in this book include cautions, warnings, and safety reminders from sources believed to be reliable, and while the text has been extensively reviewed, it is your responsibility to develop and follow procedures for the safe execution of any activity you choose to do. You are also responsible for the safe handling, use, and disposal of chemicals in accordance with local and state regulations and requirements.

Safety First

- Collect and read the Materials Safety Data Sheets (MSDS) for all of the chemicals used in your experiments. MSDS's provide physical property data, toxicity information, and handling and disposal specifications for chemicals. They can be obtained upon request from manufacturers and distributors of these chemicals. In fact, MSDS's are often shipped with chemicals when they are ordered. These should be collected and made available to students, faculty, or parents for information about specific chemicals in these activities.

- Read and follow the American Chemical Society Minimum Safety Guidelines for Chemical Demonstrations. Remember that you are a role model for your students—your attention to safety will help them develop good safety habits while assuring that everyone has fun with these activities.

- Read each activity carefully and observe all safety precautions and disposal procedures. Determine and follow all local and state regulations and requirements.

- Never attempt an activity if you are unfamiliar or uncomfortable with the procedures or materials involved. Consult a high school or college chemistry teacher or an industrial chemist for advice or ask him or her to perform the activity for your class. These people are often delighted to help.

- Always practice activities yourself before using them with your class. This is the only way to become thoroughly familiar with an activity, and familiarity will help prevent potentially hazardous (or merely embarrassing) mishaps. In addition, you may find variations that will make the activity more meaningful to your students.

- Undertake activities only at the recommended grade levels and only with adult supervision.

- You, your assistants, and any students participating in the preparation for or doing of the activity must wear safety goggles if indicated in the activity and at any other time you deem necessary.

- Special safety instructions are not given for everyday classroom materials being used in a typical manner. Use common sense when working with hot, sharp, or breakable objects. Keep tables or desks covered to avoid stains. Keep spills cleaned up to avoid falls.

- When an activity requires students to smell a substance, instruct them to smell the substance as follows: hold its container approximately 6 inches from the nose and, using the free hand, gently waft the air above the open container toward the nose. Never smell an unknown substance by placing it directly under the nose. (See figure.)

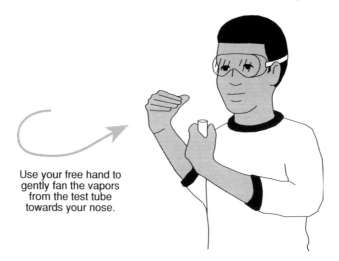

Use your free hand to gently fan the vapors from the test tube towards your nose.

Wafting procedure—Carefully wave the air above the open container towards your nose. Avoid hitting the container in the process.

- Caution students never to taste anything made in the laboratory and not to place their fingers in their mouths after handling laboratory chemicals.

ACS Minimum Safety Guidelines for Chemical Demonstrations

This section outlines safety procedures that Chemical Demonstrators must follow at all times.

1. Know the properties of the chemicals and the chemical reactions involved in all demonstrations presented.

2. Comply with all local rules and regulations.

3. Wear appropriate eye protection for all chemical demonstrations.

4. Warn the members of the audience to cover their ears whenever a loud noise is anticipated.

5. Plan the demonstration so that harmful quantities of noxious gases (e.g., NO_2, SO_2, H_2S) do not enter the local air supply.

6. Provide safety shield protection wherever there is the slightest possibility that a container, its fragments or its contents could be propelled with sufficient force to cause personal injury.

7. Arrange to have a fire extinguisher at hand whenever the slightest possibility for fire exists.

8. Do not taste or encourage spectators to taste any nonfood substance.

9. Never use demonstrations in which parts of the human body are placed in danger (such as placing dry ice in the mouth or dipping hands into liquid nitrogen).

10. Do not use "open" containers of volatile, toxic substances (e.g., benzene, CCl_4, CS_2, formaldehyde) without adequate ventilation as provided by fume hoods.

11. Provide written procedure, hazard, and disposal information for each demonstration whenever the audience is encouraged to repeat the demonstration.

12. Arrange for appropriate waste containers for and subsequent disposal of materials harmful to the environment.

Background for Teachers

This Teacher Resource Module, developed as part of the *Partners for Terrific Science* program, provides you, the teacher, with a brief overview of institutional products chemistry, an overview of Diversey Corporation's role in this industry, a Content Review, a Using the Activities in the Classroom section, and a collection of activities and demonstrations.

Overview of the Institutional Products Industry

What are institutional products? As a rule, they are similar to many consumer products that you can purchase at a supermarket or hardware store. However, institutional products are not for sale to the general public because they are often too strong or harsh for use in the home, require special application machinery, or are designed for special applications. These products are used in institutions such as hospitals, restaurants, and schools. Although most people have never heard of the companies that supply the thousands of special products used by other companies and institutions, the existence of these products affects the way we live every day.

Let's consider the kinds of situations that require special institutional products. Laundering is a good example. There are dozens of detergents and bleaches that you can buy that do a good job on clothes and linens. They are formulated for use in home washing machines. Hospitals and hotels have a very different laundry situation. They need to be able to process large quantities of linens, towels, and clothing in as short a time as possible. They use special machines which operate more quickly and at a higher temperature. The institutional detergents used in these machines are very strong and are too corrosive for use in the home machines. The cleaning of dishes, plates, and silverware present another common institutional problem. An institutional dishwasher works at a high temperatures and uses extremely caustic cleaners that wash utensils and plates in less than a minute. Moreover, a dishwasher in a hospital might use a special detergent which includes a disinfectant.

Consider another example—cleaning the floor of a walk-in freezer at a fast-food restaurant. The freezer cannot be warmed up for cleaning because the food must be kept frozen to prevent spoilage. Soap and water would freeze if used in this situation. Fortunately, institutional cleansers are available that clean without freezing at these low temperatures.

The history of the institutional products industry goes back about 100 years and parallels the consumer products industry. The differences between consumer products and institutional products often involve marketing (advertising, packaging, product appearance, etc.) as well as ingredients. A company specializing in consumer products emphasizes inventions that should appeal to millions of consumers. In order to attract potential customers, millions of dollars are spent on advertising. In contrast, a company that specializes in institutional products is usually targeting a few customers. While advertising is much less important for the institutional supplier, marketing is still important. The marketing of institutional products is achieved through a large technically knowledgeable sales team. Sales personnel able to respond quickly and efficiently to a specific customer's needs are vital. Frequently, sales are based solely on the company's ability to service an account (troubleshooting). Furthermore, retaining a team of researchers capable of quickly responding to a customer's new product needs is of vital importance. The needs of institutional products customers can change more rapidly and dramatically than those of the general public.

Overview of Diversey Corporation

This information was current as of 1995. Diversey Corporation is now JohnsonDiversey. Visit their website at www.johnsondiversey.com.

Diversey Corporation, a specialty chemical company, is a wholly-owned subsidiary of Molson Companies, Limited of Toronto, Canada. Diversey is headquartered in Mississauga, Ontario, with research support in Plymouth, Michigan, and Sharonville, Ohio. Reporting annual sales of over $1 billion, Diversey does business worldwide. Diversey sells both institutional and industrial products. The DuBois Division of Diversey Corporation is responsible for industrial products in the United States. DuBois is headquartered in Cincinnati with technical support in the Sharonville facility. DuBois lists over 700 cleaning agents, including

- cleaning agents for production equipment and other factory machines,
- steam-cleaning agents,
- rust and scale removers,
- solvent cleaners for degreasing,
- plastic cleaners,
- metal cleaners,
- drain cleaners,
- circuit board cleaners, and
- agents to clean asphalt from truck beds.

Diversey also carries a full line of water-treatment additives for commercial heating and cooling systems, including boiler-treatment additives. In addition, they offer specialty lubricants such as synthetic lubricants, polymer-enhanced lubricants, and food-grade lubricants. Another product line features iron phosphatizers for the protection of metal against corrosion and for assuring good paint adhesion.

Diversey makes plastic cleaners, such as those in the buckets above, for cleaning products such as car steering wheels and side mirrors during manufacturing. Plastic panels such as those on the right are used to test cleaners.

With so many products and such a large variety of product types, Diversey Corporation and DuBois Division dedicate an enormous effort to maintaining a professional sales staff and extensive support services. In addition, a growing number of staff are dedicated to regulatory compliance. These people make certain that all products comply with the increasing number of state and federal laws and guidelines for chemical industries.

When a customer has a unique problem or need, the salesperson communicates the need to chemists responsible for developing new products. Sometimes a new product is developed for the benefit of a single customer, with the view that more customers with similar needs will arise later. The chemists at Diversey serve in a support role for all of the products Diversey sells. If a customer has difficulty with a product, a chemist or application engineer is frequently called upon for advice. Often the problem can be solved very simply, but on rare occasions the fault lies with the product itself. Samples of every batch of every product are kept for this contingency. By studying a sample taken from the faulty batch, the chemist can often discover the source of the problem and recommend a suitable corrective action.

The Diversey Corporation Corporate Technology Centre in Sharonville, Ohio

Content Review

There are two major topics of chemistry representative of Diversey Corporation activities. They are 1) formulating mixtures and synthesizing compounds; and 2) solving some industrial cleaning problems. A brief summary of these topics, including a review of mixtures and compounds is presented here to assist you in preparing to use *Dirt Alert* activities in your classroom.

A Review of Mixtures and Compounds

Mixtures consist of two or more substances, each of which retains its individual identity. Because of this, the components of a mixture can be separated by physical means. For example, water can be evaporated from a salt-water mixture; the components of a tossed salad can be manually picked apart; and a magnet can be used to remove iron filings from a mixture of sand and iron.

There are two types of mixtures: homogeneous and heterogeneous. Homogeneous mixtures have the same composition throughout the mixture. Common examples of homogeneous mixtures include brine (a mixture of salt and water) and air (a mixture of mostly nitrogen, oxygen, argon, and carbon dioxide gases).

In contrast to homogeneous mixtures, heterogeneous mixtures have different properties in different parts. The components of the heterogeneous mixtures can be observed as individual substances. The components of a fruit salad, for example, can be easily distinguished from each other.

Because they are simple physical combinations of materials, mixtures can be formed in a variety of ratios of the individual components. As a result, it is important to know the recipe (often called the formulation) or percentage compositions for a mixture. Such formulations are often trade secrets and can be patented by the company that develops them.

Compounds are different from mixtures. Compounds are pure substances made of two or more elements chemically combined. A given compound such as sucrose (table sugar) can have only one specific chemical formula, $C_{12}H_{22}O_{11}$. The chemical formula tells us that sucrose is a compound composed of 12 carbon atoms, 22 hydrogen atoms, and 11 oxygen atoms which are chemically combined into the structure shown in Figure 1.

Figure 1: The structure of sucrose

Since the components of a compound are chemically combined rather than physically mixed, compounds cannot be separated by physical means. Instead, a chemical reaction (called a decomposition reaction) is required to separate a compound into two or more components. Figure 2 shows that heating sucrose in the absence of oxygen will form water (in the form of steam) and elemental carbon. Steam (the gaseous form of water) can be further decomposed into hydrogen and oxygen via electrolysis.

$$C_{12}H_{22}O_{11} \xrightarrow{\text{heat}} 12C + 11H_2O$$

sucrose   carbon   water

Figure 2: The decomposition of sucrose

The important characteristics that distinguish mixtures from compounds are:

- Compounds have distinctly different properties from the elements they are made from, while mixtures often retain the properties of each component of the mixture. For example, when powdered sulfur and iron filings are mixed, the iron filings are still attracted to a magnet. If iron and sulfur are heated together to a high temperature, a compound called iron sulfide is formed. Iron sulfide is not attracted to a magnet.

- A compound has a fixed ratio of elements in its composition which is expressed by its chemical formula. A mixture has no such parameters and its composition may vary greatly from sample to sample.

- Mixtures can be either homogeneous or heterogeneous, but compounds can only be homogeneous.

A solution is a type of homogeneous mixture in which the particles are of atomic, ionic, or molecular size. A solution is made from a solvent (usually the substance present in the larger amount) and a solute (the substance present in the smaller amount). A solution can have its own special characteristics which are quite different from the solvent or solute from which it is made. One of these characteristics of solutions is called freezing-point depression. Freezing-point depression is a property of a solution that gives it a lower freezing point than the pure solvent itself. The amount of the depression depends on the amount and type of the solute added.

Examples of freezing-point depression are seen frequently in our daily lives. Antifreeze (propylene glycol) is added to car radiators to prevent the cooling system from freezing during extremely cold weather. It is also the liquid that is sprayed on the wings of airplanes to deice them. The windshield wiper fluid used to clean the car's windshield is a mixture of alcohol and water. Its freezing point is lower than the freezing point of water. Calcium chloride ($CaCl_2$) is spread on icy sidewalks and streets to create a water solution with a freezing point lower than that of water. This causes the ice to melt.

Formulating Mixtures and Synthesizing Compounds

Diversey chemists are involved in the development and formulation of useful mixtures. This module includes several activities centering on the formulation of mixtures.

In the activity "Creating a Window Cleaner Company," for example, several recipes for window cleaners are provided by Diversey chemists. One is a standard formula and is similar to glass-cleaning products sold to consumers in supermarkets and discount stores. The formulation includes household ammonia, rubbing alcohol (70% isopropyl alcohol), water, and colorant which are mixed to provide a useful product. Students experiment to determine which formulation works best for cleaning windows and is the most marketable.

Another of the mixture formulations provided in this module is that for lip balm. Although Diversey does not produce a lip balm, they do sell a number of creams for institutional customers. The lip balm activity shows how common oils and waxes can be mixed to provide a useful cosmetic formulation. It is important to emphasize that no chemical reactions occur during the manufacture of the lip balm. Only physical changes occur as the ingredients are melted together and then allowed to cool.

Many recipes for similar lip balms exist in the cosmetic literature. The major ingredients are beeswax, castor oil, carnauba wax, cetyl alcohol, and lanolin. The waxes and castor oil are common cosmetic ingredients. Cetyl alcohol and lanolin are found in many lotions. These substances all have natural origins, at least historically. Lanolin is obtained from the wool of sheep, beeswax from the honeycomb of the honey bee, carnauba wax from the leaf of the Brazilian wax palm, and castor oil from the seeds of castor beans. Cetyl alcohol was originally obtained in the early 19th century from the saponification of oil from the head of the sperm whale, although it is now obtained from other sources. Small amounts of a flavored oil (oil of cinnamon, oil of wintergreen, oil of clove) or a small amount of camphor or menthol can be used to give the lip balm flavor. Oil-based food color can be added for aesthetic purposes. If desired, a trace of a food preservative, butyl p-hydroxybenzoate, can be added to prevent mold growth. Information on all of these ingredients is available in the *Merck Index*, published by Merck & Co., Inc.

In contrast to the mixtures created in the activities, the module also includes the synthesis of several different compounds that belong to the class called esters. In the "Making an Ester" activity, several different esters are made by reacting different carboxylic acids with various alcohols. These esters can be identified by their familiar odors.

Solving Some Industrial Cleaning Problems
Cleaning Products
Product development and testing are important issues associated with chemical industries. This modules includes two activities that involve students in making and testing soap products.

Pretreatment to Solve Challenging Cleaning Problems
Release agents are materials that change the nature of a surface, making it adaptable for various applications. Release agents prevent substances from sticking to surfaces and make cleanup easier. Diversey chemists have developed a release agent for use as a coating for trucks used to carry asphalt. Release agents are used to make many cleanup processes easier, including paint overspray and graffiti removal, and cleaning food from pots and pans. Release agents are used in molds in the rubber and plastics industries.

Using Sanitizing and Disinfecting Agents
In addition to wiping away grease, grime, and unwanted residues, sanitizing and disinfecting are important considerations in many cleaning products. In order to test the abilities of various cleaning agents to retard bacterial growth, Diversey microbiologists use RODAC agar plates. (RODAC is an acronym for Replicate Organism Detection and Counting.) A large number of fungi and bacteria can be cultured on these plates. An incubation time of about two or three days at room temperature is recommended. The plates are designed so that the agar gel is raised above the level of the supporting dish. This allows a sample to be obtained from a surface (to be tested for germ contamination) by lightly pressing the inverted RODAC against the surface for about 5 seconds. The RODACs are provided with a cover to prevent contamination by airborne fungi or bacteria.

RODACs are available at a nominal cost from Diversey. Similar agar plates can be obtained from many biological supply houses. Agar plates can also be homemade, although to do this properly requires some expertise. High school biology teachers, biology departments at colleges and universities, and hospital microbiology departments are resources for teachers interested in obtaining suitable agar plates.

Using the Activities in the Classroom

The activities in this module help students become aware of the importance of the institutional products industry. As they experiment with properties of lip balms and soaps and other cleaning products, they learn the role of chemistry and technology in designing effective institutional products.

Pedagogical Strategies

Anytime we can show a student how what he or she is learning in school relates to the world outside of the classroom, we help make the learning process more alive for that child. Anytime that we are able to unify different curricula, we make each curriculum stronger and more real. The activities in this module employ this strategy, enabling students to integrate their chemistry, math, language arts, and communication skills. This helps students to see chemistry not as a stagnant, isolated discipline, but rather as an integrated part of the learning experience and of the world at large. From finding the best way to clean the bread pans at a commercial bakery to deciding on the best scent for a hand cleanser or the best way to clean plastic automobile bumpers prior to painting, industrial products chemists and technicians demonstrate that chemistry is part of the "real" world.

Thematic Unit

Students know that disinfectants can clean as well as disinfect surfaces. Since students are unable to see the microorganisms or "germs" present on a given material, they can only guess whether their disinfectant is doing a good job. This unit allows them to test their preconceived ideas related to cleaning and then explore the factors important in a good cleaning agent.

The activity "Why Should We Sanitize and Disinfect?" gives students a chance to compare the effectiveness of cleaners as well as view the "germs" present on a given surface. By using agar plates to grow microorganisms, students can compare the presence of "germs" on control and disinfected surfaces. Students may be surprised to learn how many microorganisms are present on a surface they assume to be clean. They may also be surprised to find that surfaces in a bathroom that are disinfected regularly may be cleaner than surfaces located in classrooms or even their own bodies! By viewing the direct effect a disinfectant has on bacterial growth on a chosen surface, students will learn about the importance of using disinfectants.

Students can then learn the characteristics of a good cleaner or disinfectant. In activities such as "How Do We Clean Cold Surfaces?" and "Release Agents," students investigate the additives responsible for allowing cleaners to work in various environments and situations.

Once students understand the properties of a reliable cleaner, they can apply that understanding by creating their own cleaning products. In the activity "Creating a Window Cleaning Company," students formulate, package, and market their own cleaners. The process includes experimenting with and testing various product formulations to determine the most effective ones. By conducting surveys, students determine the color, packaging, and advertising needed to make their products appealing to consumers.

Individual and Group Projects

- Students can design packages for a product such as lip balm. Students may bring in empty lip balm containers which they can wash and refill with their own products, or they may choose to make their own tubes by wrapping heavy aluminum foil around a wooden dowel. The end of the tube is pinched or plugged with a cork so that warm lip balm can be poured as a liquid. Empty 35-mm film canisters can be washed and used as containers also. Once the container is chosen, students can create labels for their product.

- Students can contact local hospitals or industries and ask about special requirements they have for cleaning certain areas or equipment, such as hospital bedding, surgery rooms, or rooms where temperatures are extremely high or low. Students may also investigate what precautions are taken to prevent worker and patient exposure to "germs."

- Students can research the history of soap making and its impact on modern sanitation.

- Students may wish to investigate and collect data on the effect of a solute on the freezing point and boiling point of a liquid.

Cross-Curricular Integration

- Students can research the types of organisms involved in the transmission of disease (such as viruses and bacteria). They may wish to target a particular disease, such as pneumonia, and investigate how the invention of antibiotics and the use of disinfectants has altered the transmission, treatment, and death rate from that disease over the centuries.

- Students can research the beginning of the study of microorganisms and the use of sanitation in medicine and the effects they have had on patient death rates.

- Students can compute the growth rate of bacteria by computing their percent coverage of the agar plates. Results can then be graphed.

Annotated List of Activities and Demonstrations

To aid you in choosing activities for your classroom, we have included an annotated list of activities and demonstrations. This listing includes information about the grade level that can benefit most from an activity and a brief description of each activity. A Curriculum Placement Guide follows this list.

1. **Creating a Window Cleaner Company** (upper elementary to high school)
   Students formulate a window cleaner and package and market the cleaner just as a commercial company would. Market research surveys can be conducted to determine the color, packaging, and advertising to best appeal to the consumer.

2. **Changing the Properties of Soap** (upper elementary to high school)
   Students investigate how the properties of bar soap change when various household chemicals are added.

3. **Lip Balm** (upper elementary to high school)
   Students create lip balm from a mixture of waxes, oils, and creams. Because food grade materials are used, the lip balm that is made can actually be used.

4. **Making an Ester** (middle to high school)
   In this activity, the instructor carries out a chemical reaction between alcohols and carboxylic acids to prepare esters. These compounds have characteristic odors which are used in their identification.

5. **Making a Liquid Hand Soap** (upper elementary to high school)
   In this activity, students create a liquid hand soap which they test for lathering ability in hard water, soft water, and simulated sea water.

6. **Preparing and Testing Lard Soap** (middle to high school)
   This activity allows students to make lye soap from lard and test its properties versus a commercial brand soap.

7. **How Do We Clean Cold Surfaces?** (upper elementary to middle school)
   Using common household items such as propylene glycol (antifreeze), rubbing alcohol, salt, sugar, and water, students create mixtures that don't solidify even at 0°C.

8. **Release Agents** (upper elementary to high school)
   Ever had a cupcake stick to a baking pan or a hamburger stick to the skillet? In this activity, the students investigate the properties of certain chemicals, called release agents, which prevent substances from sticking to surfaces, and test different chemicals for their abilities to function as release agents.

9. **Why Should We Sanitize and Disinfect?** (elementary to high school)
   Students test the effectiveness of household cleaners by determining how well they disinfect surfaces. Agar plates are used as growing media for the "germ" samples.

Curriculum Placement Guide

Activities	Topics					
	Nature of Matter	Science and Technology	Scientific Method	Health	Mass, Volume, and Density	Chemical Reactivity
1 Creating a Window Cleaner Company	•	•	•		•	•
2 Changing the Properties of Soap	•	•	•	•	•	•
3 Lip Balm	•	•	•	•		•
4 Making an Ester	•	•	•	•	•	•
5 Making a Liquid Hand Soap	•	•	•	•		•
6 Preparing and Testing Lard Soap	•	•	•	•	•	•
7 How Do We Clean Cold Surfaces?	•	•	•	•		•
8 Release Agents	•	•	•	•		•
9 Why Should We Sanitize and Disinfect?	•	•	•	•		•

Activities and Demonstrations

Creating a Window Cleaner Company

What makes a commercial window cleaner work so well? Is it possible to make a similar window cleaner in the classroom? Which is more economical, the homemade cleaner or the commercial brand? Why are most window cleaners blue? These questions and more may be raised and then answered when the following activity is performed in your classroom. This activity also introduces students to some key aspects of the retail world.

Recommended Grade Level	Part 1: 4–6; Part 2: 7–12
Group Size	3–4 students
Time for Preparation	none
Time for Procedure	45–60 minutes

Materials

Opening Strategy
- bottle of commercial window cleaner

Procedure, Part 1
Per Group
- small spray bottle
- hand mirror
- dry-erase marker
- oil, grease, or dirt
- 50-mL graduated cylinder
- cotton swabs
- goggles

Per Class
- 300 mL (2 cups) rubbing alcohol (70% isopropyl alcohol solution)
- 300 mL (2 cups) water (distilled, if available)
- 60 mL (¼ cup) household ammonia
- small funnel

Procedure, Part 2
Per Group
- 50-mL graduated cylinder
- small funnel
- (optional) food color
- small spray bottle
- markers and labels
- cotton swabs
- hand mirror
- several brands of commercial window cleaner
- goggles

Per Class
- 140 mL rubbing alcohol
- 140 mL water (distilled, if available)
- 25 mL household ammonia

Variation
Per Class
- (optional) paper towels

Extensions
Per Class
- 10 mL nonfoaming surfactant (such as Photo-Flo, a non-sudsing surfactant used in photo developing)

Resources

Dry-erase markers can be purchased from office supply stores. Photo-Flo can be purchased from photography supply stores.

Safety and Disposal

Students and teachers must wear goggles at all times during the preparation and testing of the window cleaner because it contains ammonia. Household ammonia and its vapors can damage the eyes. It is recommended that contact lenses not be worn when working with ammonia because gaseous vapors may condense on the contact lens and damage the eye. Use ammonia only in a well-ventilated area. Keep the container closed when not in immediate use. Should contact with the eyes occur, rinse the affected area with water for 15 minutes, and seek medical attention while rinsing is occurring.

Isopropyl alcohol is intended for external use only. Discard all solutions used in this activity by flushing them down the drain with water.

Getting Ready

1. Ask students to bring in empty window cleaner bottles.

2. (optional) Do Part 1, Step 1, of the Procedure for the students.

Opening Strategy

Using a bottle of commercial window cleaner, wash part of a window in the classroom. Engage the students in a brainstorming session to suggest possible ingredients of the window cleaner. List these ideas and discuss the properties of the materials that would make them potential additives. Possible responses include soap (cleans, but is foamy), water (the universal solvent, but does not work well on grease), ammonia and vinegar (good grease cutters), and alcohol (a wetting agent and an antifreeze, especially for windshield washer fluid). If the ingredients are listed, read the label to reveal the actual contents of the window cleaner (usually water, isopropyl alcohol, ammonia, and colorant.)

Inform the class that they will be challenged to develop and market a new and improved window cleaner. Discuss the underlying theme that business wants to make money and one of the best ways to do that is to offer the consumer a product that is lower in cost than the competitor's brand.

Procedure

It is recommended that students work in cooperative groups in carrying out this activity.

Part 1: Testing a Window Cleaning Formula

⚠ **Observe proper safety precautions when handling ammonia solutions. See Safety and Disposal.**

1. If not prepared in Getting Ready, prepare a batch of "Original" window cleaner by mixing the ingredients listed in Table 1 in a small spray bottle. Label the spray bottle as "Original" window cleaner. This can be done by the teacher as a demonstration or by each group of students.

Table 1: Recipe for "Original Window Cleaner"

Ingredients	Amount Needed for Batch Made by Teacher	Amount Needed for Batch Made by Student	Approximate % by Volume
water	300 mL (1¼ cup)	30 mL (2 Tbsp)	45
rubbing alcohol	300 mL (1¼ cup)	30 mL (2 Tbsp)	45
household ammonia	60 mL (¼ cup)	5 mL (1 tsp)	10
total volume	660 mL (2¾ cups)	65 mL (¼+ cup)	100

2. Using a dry-erase marker, divide the surface of a hand mirror in half, labeling one side A and the other side B. Make both sides of the mirror dirty by applying a very small amount of dirt, grease, and finger smudges.

3. Using cotton swabs, wash side A with the "Original" window cleaner and side B with a commercial brand. Measure the amount of cleaner (i.e., the number of sprays), the number of cotton swabs, and the number of strokes used for each half of the mirror and record the observations.

4. Examine sides A and B and decide which window cleaner cleaned the mirror best by rubbing a dry cotton swab over each side of the mirror and examining the end for residual dirt. (If there is no difference between the amount of dirt remaining on the mirror surface after both cleaners, this shows that the "Original" window cleaner was as effective as the commercial brand in its cleaning power. You may want to address the issue of cost since both cleaners have similar cleaning abilities.)

Part 2: Developing a "New and Improved" Window Cleaning Formula

⚠ **Because of the use of concentrated reagents, this part is not recommended for students in lower grades.**

1. Assign each group a different "recipe" for window cleaner from Table 2. (Older students may wish to devise their own recipes.)

Table 2: Approved Recipes for Window Cleaner

Recipe	Water	Rubbing Alcohol	Ammonia
Standard	25 mL (45%)	25 mL (45%)	5 mL (10%)
Variation 1	25 mL (50%)	25 mL (50%)	—
Variation 2	40 mL (80%)	—	10 mL (20%)
Variation 3	50 mL (100%)	—	—
Variation 4	—	50 mL (100%)	—
Variation 5	—	40 mL (80%)	10 mL (20%)

2. Pour the appropriate window cleaner ingredients into a small spray bottle using the funnel and mix them thoroughly by swirling. If desired, add 1–3 drops of food color. Label the bottle "New and Improved" window cleaner.

3. Develop a method for testing the window cleaner against commercial brands. Make sure to consider the amount of window cleaner used, the number of cotton swabs used, and the number of strokes used to clean each half of the window or mirror.

4. Ask the students how they could prove their window cleaner did a satisfactory job. Have them evaluate their group's formulation against other groups' formulations.

5. Provide unit cost information for each of the ingredients and have each group develop a cost comparison of their product and a commercial product.

6. Record on the board the test data for each recipe and the commercial brands. Rank the different window cleaner recipes and the commercial brands in order from most effective to least effective. Include the cost analysis with each recipe and the commercial brand.

Part 3: Marketing a Window Cleaner

1. Discuss what would be needed before the "New and Improved" window cleaner could be sold in the grocery store. Mention topics such as safety of use, compliance with industrial and governmental standards, environmentally friendly ingredients, consumer appeal, product name and label design, and consumer cost.

2. Decide on a target population for product development. Discuss the cost aspect of the product as a reason for possibly changing the "New and Improved" formula so that it is less expensive to produce.

3. Explain that the name of the window cleaner should appeal to those who purchase it. Challenge groups to develop marketing strategies and possible names for their "New and Improved" window cleaners. Groups should narrow the list down to the three best names.

4. Develop a market survey to determine which of the three names is best and which color best represents clean and fresh.

5. Prepare mock window cleaner solutions of various colors to use in the market survey.

6. For homework, each member of the group should ask 10 potential buyers to complete the survey.

7. The group members should share results of their surveys and come to a consensus for the name and color of the window cleaner.

8. Do a cost analysis for the product to determine the selling price necessary to break even or make a profit.

Variation

- In Parts 1 and 2, instead of cleaning the surface of the mirror with cotton swabs, establish a standard cleaning method which each group of students will use while testing their window cleaner versus the commercial window cleaner. One standard method that has been suggested is the following: 1) Apply two sprays of cleaner to each test area; and 2) Wipe each test area 3–4 times in the same direction with a single paper towel using moderate pressure.

Extensions

- Prepare a Product Testing Analysis statement comparing the "New and Improved" formulation to the "Original" formula and the commercial brand.

- Develop an advertising scheme and commercial for the product.

- Experiment with the recipe for the "New and Improved" formula by adding a small quantity (5% or less) of a surfactant (e.g., Photo-Flo). Determine whether this formulation leaves more or less residue than other formulations.

- Consider issues regarding the product's stability after manufacture. Will the consumer need to "shake well before using"? In hot weather? In cold?

- Discuss ways of reducing the cost of the homemade product, e.g., Can the "Original" cleaner be diluted with water and still be effective compared to the commercial brand? If so, this is a simple way to reduce cost.

Discussion

- Ask students which recipe cleaned the mirrors best and how effective the criteria used to determine the "best" were.

- Ask students why water is the main ingredient in many window cleaner recipes.
  Water is the least expensive ingredient in a window cleaner formula so manufacturers make it the main ingredient to keep costs down.

- Ask students why commercial brands of window cleaners cost so much more than the homemade window cleaners.
  Advertising is the most expensive item in the budget of a commercial window cleaner. Other costs the commercial window cleaner has that were not factored into the cost of the homemade cleaners are a) manufacturing/producing overhead (including electricity, heat, water, and maintenance of the building); b) cost of labor; and c) transportation of the product to distributors.

Explanation

Many commercial window cleaners use formulas similar to the "Original" formula used in this activity. Each manufacturer adds certain ingredients to make its product unique. Colors and scents (which add to cost significantly) and active ingredients (e.g., ammonia, vinegar, alcohol, and various soaps) differ from one product to another. Most major companies use ammonia as the grease-cutting agent. While vinegar could also be used for this purpose, ammonia is less expensive. Although the cost difference between the two is typically in the range of only several cents per gallon, this amounts to a large total savings considering that millions of gallons of window cleaner are produced each year.

An ammonia-containing window cleaner "cuts" grease as a result of a chemical reaction between the aqueous ammonia and the grease. This reaction is shown by the general equation in Figure 1. The reaction is called a hydrolysis reaction and involves water in the presence of the base ammonia reacting with triglycerides which are found in the grease. The products of this reaction are glycerol and water-soluble salts of the fatty acids. A similar hydrolysis reaction is used to make soap. Acids, such as vinegar or lemon juice, can be acceptable substitutes for the ammonia because they cause a similar hydrolysis of fats and oils.

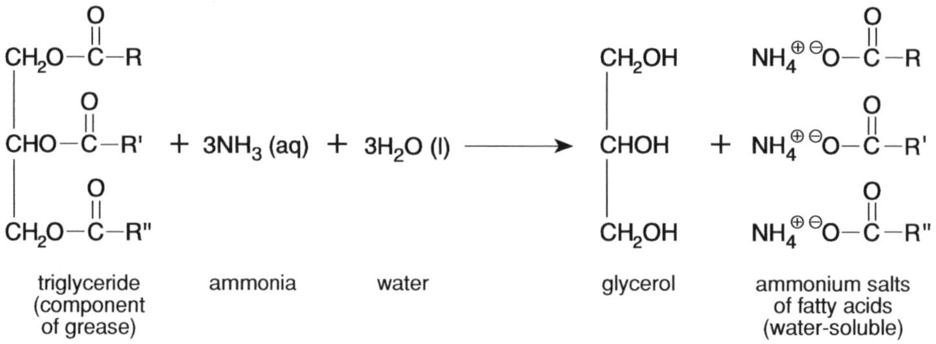

Figure 1: The hydrolysis reaction between ammonia and a fat

A mixture of water and isopropyl alcohol typically serves as the solvent in the window cleaner. The volatility of the alcohol solution allows for evaporation. This solvent lifts the dust and dirt as well as the products of the hydrolysis reaction previously outlined. Once these materials are suspended in the water/alcohol solution, they can easily be wiped from the surface of the glass.

As in the third extension, surfactants like Photo-Flo (a non-sudsing surfactant used in photo developing) are sometimes used in window cleaners. These surfactants help reduce the surface tension of the water, making it easier to wet the surface, an important aspect of cleaning. Additionally these surfactants help to remove grease and oils in much the same way detergents clean clothes.

Key Science Concepts

- hydrolysis of grease and oils
- solubility

Cross-Curricular Integration

Language Arts
Design an advertisement to sell students' "New and Improved" window cleaner. You may even want to videotape the ad.

Mathematics
Graph the test data from each group using a histogram or line graph.

Reference

Sarquis, A.M; et al. "Creating a Window Cleaner Company," *Journal of Chemical Education*. 1995, 72(4), 344–345.

Changing the
Properties of Soap

Why do most facial soaps contain glycerol (glycerin)? How do additives affect a soap's properties? Can you substitute other chemicals for the glycerol and still have a good soap? Students investigate how the properties of bar soap change when various household chemicals are added.

Recommended Grade Level **4–12**
Group Size .... **1–4 students**
Time for Preparation .... **20–25 minutes**
Time for Procedure .... **30–35 minutes (+ several days for drying non-glycerol soap formulas)**

Materials

Opening Strategy
- bar of Ivory® soap

Procedure, Part 1
Per Group
- 20 g (½ cup) Ivory bar soap
- 15 mL rubbing alcohol (70% isopropyl alcohol solution)
- 25 mL glycerol, plus some for coating molds
- mold for the soap (e.g., plastic weighing boat, aluminum foil pressed inside a beaker or cup, a wax-coated cup, etc.)
- 250-mL beaker
- 50-mL graduated cylinder
- stirring rod
- (optional) food color
- (optional) fragrance oil (e.g., oil of cinnamon, oil of clove, etc.)
- (optional) zipper-type plastic bag
- goggles

Per Class
- cheese graters
- balances
- 1 of the following sources of heat:
   - hot plates (stirring model with magnetic stir bar, if available)
   - Bunsen burners, ring stands, ring clamps, and wire gauze

Procedure, Part 2
Per Group
Materials listed for Part 1 plus 25 mL of 1 of the following:
- corn syrup
- baby oil
- mineral oil

- 50/50 baby oil/glycerol mixture
- 50/50 mineral oil/glycerol mixture
- propylene glycol

Variation

Per Group
Materials listed for Part 1 plus the following:
- several different kinds of bar soaps

Resources

Glycerol, propylene glycol, and mineral oil can be purchased from chemical supply companies. (See Chemical Supply Companies at the end of this book.)

Glycerol, Ivory bar soap, rubbing alcohol, fragrances, baby oil, mineral oil, and corn syrup can be purchased from pharmacies and grocery stores.

Safety and Disposal

Goggles should be worn when performing this activity. All chemicals used in this activity are intended for external use only.

Getting Ready

For younger students, you may wish to grate the Ivory bar soap ahead of time and place it in labeled, zipper-type plastic bags.

Opening Strategy

Show the students a bar of Ivory soap in its package and ask the students if they know what it is. Have them list several of its properties. *White in color, pleasant smell, floats in water, etc.* Have the students wash their hands with the Ivory soap and describe how it feels and how well it cleans. Ask them to suggest ways in which they could change the properties of the soap. *Heat the soap, add something to the soap, etc.*

Procedure

Part 1: Making Glycerol Soap

1. Using a cheese grater, grate approximately 20 g (½ cup) of Ivory bar soap and pour it into the 250-mL beaker.

2. Add 15 mL rubbing alcohol (70% isopropyl alcohol solution), 25 mL glycerol, and 15 mL water to the grated soap.

3. Stir the mixture continually over low heat until a clear, thick solution is obtained.

4. (optional) Add 2–3 drops each of food color and fragrance oil.

5. Prepare the mold for the soap by coating the inside of the mold with a thin layer of glycerol.

6. Pour the mixture into the mold and allow it to cool and harden overnight.

7. Remove the soap from the mold and wash your hands with it. Compare the glycerol soap to the pure Ivory soap considering how they feel and how well they clean. Record any observations.

Part 2: Why Glycerol?

1. Repeat Part 1, Steps 1–6, substituting 25 mL of one of the following liquids for the glycerol: corn syrup, baby oil, mineral oil, propylene glycol, a 50/50 baby oil/glycerol mixture, or a 50/50 mineral oil/glycerol mixture.

 Some of the soap mixtures will not solidify overnight. It may take several days before they will be hard enough for the students to handle.

2. Remove soap from the mold and wash your hands with it. Compare the new soap to the glycerol soap and to pure Ivory soap. Record the results.

Variation

- Repeat Part 1 substituting different brands of bar soap for the Ivory soap. Some examples of bar soaps that make interesting glycerol soaps are Lava® (with pumice), castile soap (good for hard water areas), and deodorant soaps. Many of these soap mixtures also do not solidify overnight. It may take several days for them to harden enough for students to handle them.

Discussion

- Discuss the effect of adding glycerol on the appearance of the soap mixture.
  The opaque mixture becomes clear or only slightly cloudy.

- Discuss the differences between washing hands with the glycerol soap and washing with the Ivory soap.
  The glycerol soap is a milder soap that doesn't dry out hands as much as the Ivory soap. The natural oils removed by the soap are replaced with a layer of glycerol that protects hands and keeps them from becoming dry.

- Discuss the differences in appearance and feel of the soaps produced in Part 2 versus the glycerol soap made in Part 1.
  Soaps made from propylene glycol and corn syrup were similar in appearance to the glycerol soap. (Both were clear except that the corn syrup soap had an opaque, foamy skin on top.) The baby oil and mineral oil soaps were both opaque and had foamy skins on top which held excess oil. The only difference between these two was the scent; baby oil is simply mineral oil with fragrance added. The corn syrup soap was sticky to the touch but lathered quite well. Both oil soaps were oily feeling and did not lather very well. The propylene glycol soap was the closest in feel and lather to the glycerol soap. If soap was made from a 50/50 mixture of oil and glycerol, two layers are formed with the bottom layer being clear and with the top layer being very cloudy. The oil/glycerol soaps did not lather very well but left your hands feeling very soft.

Explanation

The soaps formed in this activity are mixtures containing Ivory soap, water, and other additives. The appearance and texture of the original Ivory soap is altered by the addition of glycerol, resulting in a clear, creamy soap. Glycerol soaps are considered milder than most soaps. This is because the glycerol coats the skin, replacing the natural skin oils removed by the soap in the cleaning process, and helps prevent the skin from drying out.

The type of additive used plays an important role in determining the properties of the final mixture. The molecular structures of the various additives used in the activity are shown in Figure 1. Glycerol, propylene glycol, and corn syrup (a solution of fructose and glucose) contain hydroxy functional groups (–OH); these additives enhance the solubility of the Ivory soap in the water/rubbing alcohol solution and increase the clarity of the resulting mixture. The oil additives leave the mixture more oily, but do not affect the transparency.

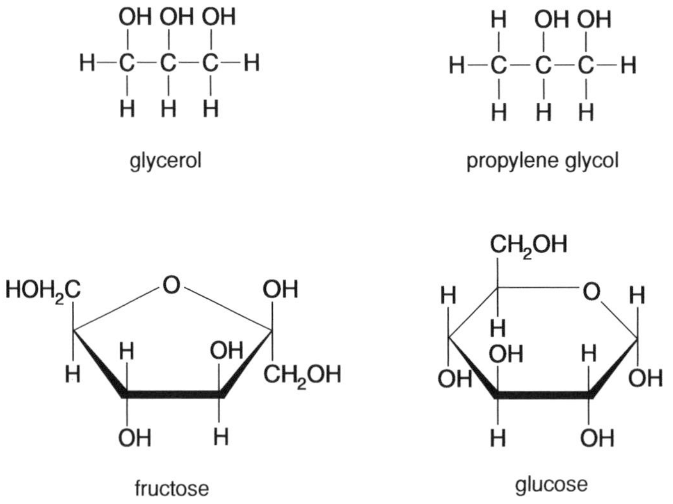

Figure 1: The structures of additives used in the soap mixture

Key Science Concepts

- mixtures
- physical/chemical changes

Cross-Curricular Integration

Language Arts
Have the students write commercials or slogans to market their glycerol soap and its properties.

Life Science
Discuss the use of soap in personal hygiene and disease prevention.

Social Studies
Have the students investigate the preparation of soap in different cultures or over different periods in history.

Lip Balm

What chemicals are used to make lip balm? How is it made? In this activity, students make their own lip balm and may be surprised to find that the product they make works just as well as most commercial ones.

Recommended Grade Level **5–12**
Group Size .... **3–5 students**
Time for Preparation .... **none**
Time for Procedure .... **40–60 minutes**

Materials

Opening Strategy
- several common brands of lip balm
- castor oil
- lanolin
- 1 or more of the following:
  - beeswax
  - carnauba wax
  - cetyl alcohol (hexadecanol)
- (optional) butyl p-hydroxybenzoate

Procedure
Per Group
- 5 g (1 Tbsp) carnauba wax
- 8 g (1 Tbsp) beeswax
- 3 g (1 tsp) lanolin
- 2.5 g (a little less than 1 tsp) cetyl alcohol (hexadecanol)
- 45 mL (3 Tbsp) castor oil
- (optional) 1 of the following flavors:
  - 1 g (½ tsp) camphor
  - 0.5 mL (10 drops) oil of cinnamon or other oil-based flavor
- (optional) 0.25 mg butyl p-hydroxybenzoate
- hot plate
- small saucepan
- spoon
- masking tape and marking pen for labels
- spatula
- commercial lip balms
- 1 of the following lip balm containers for each student:
  - 35-mm film canister
  - 2-oz ointment bottle
- measuring spoons
- (optional) ice bath
- goggles

Variations

- 1 or both of the following:
  - ◦ oil-based food colors
  - ◦ commercial oil-based flavor (e.g., oil of wintergreen, oil of clove)

Resources

Carnauba wax, beeswax, lanolin, cetyl alcohol, camphor, ointment bottles, and butyl p-hydroxybenzoate can be purchased from chemical supply companies such as Sigma-Aldrich, St. Louis, MO; 800/325-3010; *http://www.sigmaaldrich.com*. (See Chemical Supply Companies at the end of this book.)

Castor oil can be purchased from pharmacies. Oil of cinnamon, as well as other oil-based flavors, can be purchased from some supermarkets and gourmet food shops.

Safety and Disposal

Goggles should be worn when performing this activity.

Clean equipment and utensils must be used as if food were being prepared. The materials used in this activity are intended for external use only. Students should wash their hands after touching the lip balm. Persons with especially sensitive skin or known allergies to any of the lip balm ingredients should avoid contact with the lip balm. Caution students to handle hot liquids with care. The compounds used in this activity can be safely discarded in the trash.

Opening Strategy

Purchase several common brands of lip balms and pass them around the room. Tell the students to smell the samples and to rub some on their hands to feel the texture.

 To avoid spreading germs, do not allow students to try the sample on their lips.

Pass a small amount of each major ingredient around the room. The castor oil can be passed around in its container, a bit of lanolin can be passed around on a piece of paper towel and bits of wax (beeswax, carnauba wax, and cetyl alcohol) can be handled directly, then discarded.

If the preservative butyl p-hydroxybenzoate is being used, show a sample of the powder to the students. Explain that it is used to prevent spoiling and that it is similar to other preservatives used to extend the shelf life of bread and other store-bought foods.

Ask students if they know where any of these materials come from and some uses for each component (besides in lip balm).

Procedure

1. Measure each of the five ingredients listed below and place them into a small pan to melt.
   - ◦ 5 g (1 Tbsp) carnauba wax
   - ◦ 8 g (1 Tbsp) beeswax
   - ◦ 3 g (1 tsp) lanolin
   - ◦ 2.5 g (about 1 tsp) cetyl alcohol (hexadecanol)
   - ◦ 45 mL (3 Tbsp) castor oil

2. Warm the pan gently on the hot plate until the ingredients melt completely. Mix the ingredients by gently stirring with a spoon.

3. If the butyl p-hydroxybenzoate is being used, add about 0.25 mg (a very small "pinch") to the pan and stir gently.

4. If a flavoring is being used, add approximately 1 g (a medium pinch) camphor or 5 drops of oil of cinnamon and stir for about 1 minute.

5. Pour equal amounts of the liquid into each container (one for each student in the group) and allow to cool. Label each container with a name for identification. If desired, a product name, a list of ingredients, or any other decorations can also be added to the label. **A film canister ¼ full takes about 5 minutes to harden; a canister ½ full takes about 15 minutes. Placing the canister in an ice bath helps the lip balm harden faster.**

Persons with especially sensitive skin or a known skin allergy to any of the lip balm ingredients should avoid contact with the lip balm.

6. Make observations about the lip balm using the senses of touch, smell, and sight. Compare the homemade lip balm to commercial lip balms.

Variations

- Make a batch of lip balm with and without the preservative butyl p-hydroxybenzoate. Observe the product over several months.

- Experiment with the lip balm recipe to improve it. Oil-based food colors (available from cake decorating and candy supply shops) can be added to improve the appearance of the lip balm. Commercial oil-based flavors, such as oil of wintergreen or oil of clove, used in candy making, are acceptable substitutes for the camphor or oil of cinnamon.

Extension

- Form an imaginary cosmetics company and discuss issues related to developing and marketing a lip balm such as packaging, product names, product improvements, consumer costs, etc.

Discussion

- Ask the students to classify the lip balm as a compound or a mixture.
  The lip balm is a mixture because the ingredients did not undergo any chemical change such as production of a gas or formation of water.

- Ask the students to explain why lip balm helps to relieve chapped lips.
  Chapping results from lip cells becoming dehydrated. The lip balm is made of waxy substances which forms a water-resistant barrier when applied to the lips. The moisture from the lip cells cannot escape, therefore preventing further chapping of the lips.

Explanation

In the cosmetic industry, the word "compounding" is used to describe the mixing of two or more chemicals to obtain a finished product. Since no chemical changes occur, the resulting product, despite the name of the process, is a mixture and not a compound in the chemical sense of the word.

A lip balm has a number of stringent requirements. It must not contain any toxic substances. It must be hard enough to maintain its shape in hot weather, yet soft enough to be easily applied to the lips. It must also provide a moisture-proof barrier to prevent the lips from drying. The balm may also contain oils or medications to soften the skin and promote healing. The oils and waxes used in this activity to make the lip balm are all naturally occurring. Their sources are listed in Table 1.

Table 1: Sources of Oils and Waxes

Oil or Wax	Source
carnauba wax	This wax is exuded by the leaves of the Brazilian wax palm tree and is used in many personal hygiene products such as stick deodorants. It is also used to make high-quality car wax.
beeswax	This wax is formed in the honeycomb of the honeybee and is used extensively as a foundation for ointments and cosmetics.
lanolin	This compound is a fat-like secretion of sheep which is deposited on the wool. It is commonly used as an ointment base in pharmaceuticals and hand lotions.
cetyl alcohol	This compound was originally obtained in the 19th century by treating oil extracted from the head of the sperm whale with lye. It is now synthesized in the laboratory and is commonly used in cosmetics.
castor oil	This oil is extracted by cold-pressing the seeds of the castor oil plant and is used as a lubricant in many cosmetics. It is perhaps most notorious for its use as a purgative to relieve constipation.

Two minor components may be added to enhance the quality of the lip balm. Camphor, a product of the camphor tree, imparts a pleasant odor and a tingling sensation when the lip balm is applied to the lips. A trace of butyl p-hydroxybenzoate prevents mold growth. This preservative is produced naturally in a modified form by *Penicillium patulum*.

Key Science Concepts

- compounding
- cosmetic chemistry
- mixtures

Cross-Curricular Integration

Home, Safety, and Career

Compare and contrast various brands of popular cosmetics (including lip balms) used by students in order to assess how well these products achieve their respective advertising claims.

Making an Ester

Manufacturers often add pleasant scents to cleaning products to make them more appealing to consumers. Many natural and artificial scents belong to a class of compounds called esters. Esters are produced by a chemical process called esterification, and in this activity, students will observe as the instructor prepares several synthetic scents that are esters. Students will have the opportunity to smell the esters that are produced.

> **Recommended Grade Level** 7–12
> **Group Size** .... demonstration
> **Time for Preparation** .... 30 minutes
> **Time for Procedure** .... 25 minutes (+ 20 minutes for heating)

Materials

Getting Ready
- film canisters or other small opaque containers with plastic lids (1 container for each ester made)
- pushpin
- (optional) extra plastic lids
- (optional) zipper-type freezer bags

Procedure
For Each Ester Being Prepared
- 0.2 g (a large pinch) Dowex® 50W X 2-100 cation exchange resin beads
- medium-sized test tube (e.g., 13-mm or 16-mm by 150-mm)
- 2–3 small boiling stone
- ½ tsp potassium carbonate (K_2CO_3)
- 1 of the alcohol/carboxylic acid pairs shown in Table 1
- cotton ball

Per Class
- sand bath made from the following:
  - fine, clean sand (e.g., fine play sand)
  - 150- or 250-mL beaker or similar glass container
- hot plate
- alcohol or metal thermometer that reads at least as high as 120°C
- goggles
- tongs, heat-resistant mitt, or hot pad

Variation
- several balloons
- food flavorings
- string

Resources

The chemicals for this activity can be purchased from chemical supply companies. (See Chemical Supply Companies at the end of this book.)

Dowex 50W X 2-100 cation exchange resin can be purchased from Sigma-Aldrich, St. Louis, MO; 800/325-3010; *http://www.sigmaaldrich.com.*

Safety and Disposal

Conduct the class demonstration in a well-ventilated area under a fume hood. Wear goggles, gloves, and an apron when performing this demonstration. All of the alcohols used in this activity are flammable and should be kept away from open flames or hot plates.

Methanol (also called wood alcohol) is very toxic if ingested and can be absorbed through the skin. If contact occurs, rinse the affected area with water.

Glacial acetic acid and formic acid are dangerous if they come in contact with the skin or their vapors are inhaled. These substances should be handled only by the instructor. Avoid smelling these acids or unreacted mixtures containing them, even with the wafting technique, due to the strong odors and the possibility of dropping the containers during the process.

When the students smell the final esters in the activity, instruct them to wear goggles and to use the wafting technique. Instruct students never to taste these or any products that have been made in the laboratory, as the crude esters synthesized in this activity may contain significant amounts of toxic impurities.

Rinse solutions down the drain with plenty of water. When disposing of the container contents, pour liquid down the drain with the running water. Dump solids into a plastic bag, tie off, and discard.

Getting Ready

Label each opaque container with the esters you will be making during the class demonstration. Poke 20–30 holes in the lids with a pushpin to prepare scent-diffusing lids.

If class time does not permit the 20-minute warming step, prepare the esters before class and place them in the labeled containers as described in Step 6. To avoid cross-contaminating odors, put solid lids on the containers and store them separately in secondary sealed containers like zipper-type freezer bags.

Procedure

Do Steps 1–6 as a class demonstration.

1. Prepare a sand bath by filling enough 150-mL or 250-mL beakers halfway with sand to hold all of test tubes you will use. Warm the beaker(s) to 120°C with a hot plate. While the sand is warming, continue with Steps 2–4.

2. For each ester being made, place about 0.2 g (a large pinch) Dowex 50W X 2-100 resin beads into a test tube.

3. Prepare one or more of the alcohol/carboxylic acid pairs listed in Table 1. Add the correct amounts of alcohol and carboxylic acid to the resin beads in each test tube.

Table 1: Alcohol/Carboxylic Acid Pairs and Resulting Esters

Alcohol	Carboxylic Acid	Ester	Odor of Ester
20 drops methanol	0.5 g salicylic acid (about a half pea-sized amount)	methyl salicylate	wintergreen
10 drops isobutanol	10 drops formic acid	isobutyl formate	raspberry
10 drops isoamyl alcohol	30 drops glacial acetic acid	isoamyl acetate	banana
10 drops octanol	30 drops glacial acetic acid	octyl acetate	bitter orange (citrus, orange)
10 drops n-propanol	30 drops glacial acetic acid	n-propyl acetate	pear

You will need to heat the methanol/salicylic acid pair differently than the other pairs. Methanol boils at about 65°C and will spurt out of the test tube if placed in the sand bath for the allotted time of the procedure. Instead, heat the methanol/salicylic acid in a test tube immersed in a beaker of very hot (just below 100°C) water.

4. Add two or three small boiling stones to each test tube to help prevent the contents of the test tubes from frothing during the heating step that follows.

5. Stand the test tubes in the sand bath that has been warmed to 100–120°C. Allow the test tubes to heat for at least 20 minutes.

Heating for at least 20 minutes is required to produce noticeable levels of the characteristic ester odors. An hour or more of heating may be required for the reactants to be completely consumed. The potassium carbonate added in Step 6 is intended to neutralize any unreacted acid.

Each test tube and its contents will be hot.

6. After about 20 minutes of heating, use tongs, a heat-resistent mitt, or a hot pad to decant the liquid from each test tube into a separate canister containing ½ tsp potassium carbonate (K_2CO_3). (It's okay if the boiling stones or Dowex resin beads fall into the canister.) Put a cotton ball in each canister on top of the mixture. Place a scent-diffusing lid on each container.

7. Review the wafting technique with the students. Ask students to pass the containers around the classroom so everyone can smell the esters. Instruct students not to open or tip over these containers. Ask students to use the wafting technique to smell the contents of each container. If the odor is not strong enough to identify, students may smell the lid directly, but should not remove the lid from the container.

Variation

- Provide some commercial esters (or food flavorings) for the students to smell by placing a few drops of each into a separate balloon. Inflate the balloon and tie the end. Pass the balloons around the class to see if students can identify the odor. Have them compare these flavorings with the compounds formed in the activity. Make a chart on the blackboard and pool the class results. Reiterate the concept that these odors are chemicals and explain that many chemicals that have strong odors belong to a class of chemicals called esters.

Discussion

- Describe and compare the odors of the esters your teacher made.
  The odors of each ester are listed in Table 1: Alcohol/Carboxylic Acid Pairs and Resulting Esters.

- In this activity, the Dowex resin acts as a catalyst. What is the purpose of a catalyst?
  A catalyst is a substance that speeds up the rate of a reaction.

- Copy down the chemical structures for the alcohols and carboxylic acids used in the class demonstration. What esters were made? What small molecule was eliminated when the two starting reagents were combined and the ester was made?
  Table 2 shows the chemical structure for each alcohol, carboxylic acid, and ester from the class demonstration. Water was eliminated from the two starting reagents during each esterification process.

Table 2: Chemical Structures of Reagents and Their Esters

Acid	Carboxylic Acid	Resulting Ester	Odor of Ester
methanol CH_3-OH	salicylic acid	methyl salicylate	wintergreen
isobutanol $CH_3-CH-CH_2-OH$ (with CH_3 branch)	formic acid $HO-CH=O$	isobutyl formate $CH_3-CH-CH_2-O-CH=O$ (with CH_3 branch)	raspberry
isoamyl alcohol $H_3C-CH-CH_2-CH_2-OH$ (with CH_3 branch)	glacial acetic acid $HO-C-CH_3$ (with $=O$)	isoamyl acetate $H_3C-CH-CH_2-CH_2-O-C-CH_3$ (with CH_3 branch, $=O$)	banana
octanol $CH_3-(CH_2)_7-OH$	glacial acetic acid $HO-C-CH_3$ (with $=O$)	octyl acetate $CH_3-(CH_2)_7-O-C-CH_3$ (with $=O$)	orange
n-propanol $CH_3-CH_2-CH_2-OH$	glacial acetic acid $HO-C-CH_3$ (with $=O$)	n-propyl acetate $CH_3-CH_2-CH_2-O-C-CH_3$ (with $=O$)	pear

Explanation

An ester is formed when a carboxylic acid reacts with an alcohol in a process known as esterification. (See Figure 1.) During the esterification, the –OH group from the acid combines with a –H functional group from the alcohol, forming H_2O. This reaction typically requires a catalyst to speed it. For decades, concentrated sulfuric acid ($18\,M\ H_2SO_4$) has been used for this purpose, as it is a strong dehydrating agent. However, for the same reason, it is very dangerous to use. It can cause severe chemical burns that result from the dehydration of the proteins in your skin.

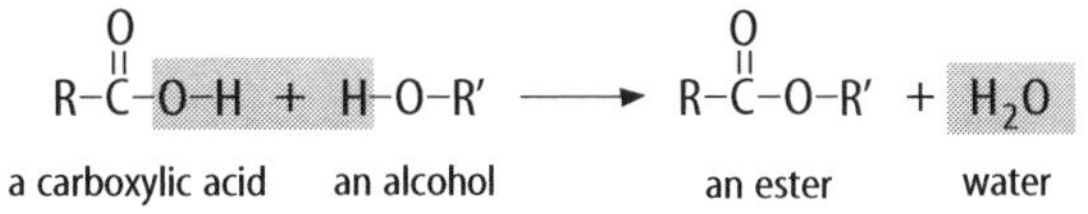

$$\underset{\text{a carboxylic acid}}{R-\overset{\overset{\displaystyle O}{\|}}{C}-O-H} + \underset{\text{an alcohol}}{H-O-R'} \longrightarrow \underset{\text{an ester}}{R-\overset{\overset{\displaystyle O}{\|}}{C}-O-R'} + \underset{\text{water}}{H_2O}$$

Figure 1: The reaction of a carboxylic acid with an alcohol to form an ester (R and R' represent long carbon chains.) (Shading shows water loss.)

The procedure suggested for this activity uses a relatively new and safer acidic material called a cation exchange resin; its trade name is Dowex 50W X 2-100, and it is manufactured by the Dow Chemical Company. The Dowex resin acts just as the concentrated sulfuric acid does by scavenging the water produced by the esterification reaction and drives the reaction toward producing the ester. The potassium carbonate (K_2CO_3) neutralizes any excess acid remaining after the reaction. The equation for the esterification of glacial acetic acid and isoamyl alcohol to make isoamyl acetate (the odor of bananas) is shown in Figure 2.

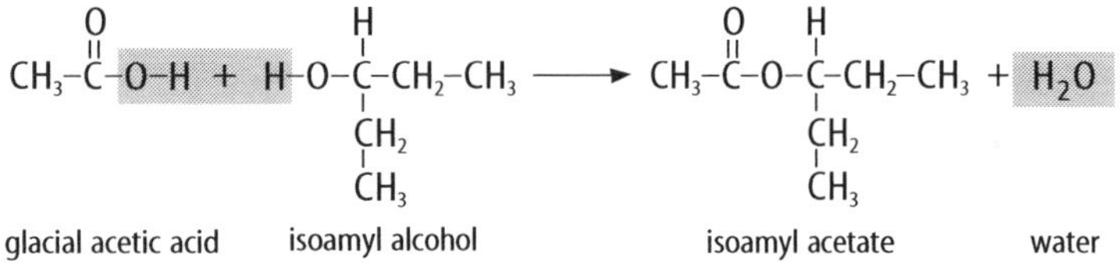

$$\underset{\text{glacial acetic acid}}{CH_3-\overset{\overset{\displaystyle O}{\|}}{C}-O-H} + \underset{\text{isoamyl alcohol}}{H-O-\overset{\overset{\displaystyle H}{|}}{\underset{\underset{CH_3}{\overset{|}{CH_2}}}{\underset{|}{C}}}-CH_2-CH_3} \longrightarrow \underset{\text{isoamyl acetate}}{CH_3-\overset{\overset{\displaystyle O}{\|}}{C}-O-\overset{\overset{\displaystyle H}{|}}{\underset{\underset{CH_3}{\overset{|}{CH_2}}}{\underset{|}{C}}}-CH_2-CH_3} + \underset{\text{water}}{H_2O}$$

Figure 2: Esterification to make isoamyl acetate (odor of banana) (Shading shows water loss.)

When low-molecular-weight carboxylic acids are esterified, the resulting esters are typically colorless liquids with fruity odors. These synthetic esters are used in the food industry as flavorings and in other industries as scents. In many cases, the esters produced in the laboratory are the same molecules that give fruits their characteristic flavors and odors. For example, isoamyl acetate, the chemical that gives bananas their characteristic flavor, can be made in the lab by reacting isoamyl alcohol with acetic acid. Other synthetic esters have no known natural counterparts. However, some do have characteristic fruity or sweet odors.

Key Science Concepts

- catalysts
- esters

Cross-Curricular Integration

Home, Safety, and Career
Have students look around their homes for cleaning products that might contain ester scents. Discuss why companies add scents to cleaning products. Do they help the product to clean better?

Reference

An activity dealing with the synthesis of flavors also appears in the *Science Fare* and *Fat Chance* modules of the *Science in Our World* series.

Making a Liquid Hand Soap

Most liquid hand soaps are actually detergents. In this activity students make a liquid hand soap similar to commercial liquid hand soaps and compare the properties of the homemade hand soap to those of a commercial brand.

Recommended Grade Level 4–12
Group Size .... 1–4 students
Time for Preparation .... 10 minutes
Time for Procedure .... 50–60 minutes

Materials

Opening Strategy
Per Group
- vegetable oil or shortening
- liquid hand soap

Procedure, Part 1
Per Group
- 2 pump bottles
- plastic spoon or stirring stick
- 400-mL beaker or mixing bowl
- 10-mL graduated cylinder
- 50-mL graduated cylinder
- disposable plastic pipet or dropper
- 50.0 g ammonium lauryl sulfate
- 2.0 mL lauramide diethylamine (DEA)
- 4.8 mL sodium lauryl sulfate
- 0.8 mL (16 drops) glycerol (glycerin)
- 0.3 g citric acid (anhydrous)
- 0.2 g tetrasodium ethylenediaminetetraacetic acid (sodium EDTA)
- goggles

Procedure, Part 2
Per Group
- liquid hand soap prepared in Part 1
- 3 jars with lids such as baby food jars
- 40 drops of vegetable oil
- 1 Tbsp table salt (sodium chloride, NaCl)
- 1 Tbsp calcium chloride ($CaCl_2$)
- labels
- disposable plastic pipet or dropper
- plastic spoon or stirring stick
- metric ruler

Per Class
- tap water (if soft) or distilled water
- several commercial brands of liquid hand soap and bar soap

Resources

Citric acid, calcium chloride, sodium lauryl sulfate, and tetrasodium ethylenediaminetetraacetic acid (sodium EDTA) can be purchased from chemical supply companies. (See Chemical Supply Companies at the end of this book.)

Distilled water can be purchased in 1-gallon plastic jugs from grocery stores. Calcium chloride can be purchased as sidewalk deicer from grocery and hardware stores.

Lauramide diethylamine (DEA), sodium lauryl sulfate (as sodium laureth sulfate), tetrasodium ethylenediaminetetraacetic acid (sodium EDTA), and ammonium lauryl sulfate can be ordered from Diversey Corporation, ATTN: Carol Marquardt, Cincinnati, OH; 513/554-4200; *http://www.duboischemical.com.*

Safety and Disposal

Goggles should be worn when performing this activity. The materials used in this activity are intended for external use only.

Avoid skin and eye contact with concentrated or solid ethylenediaminetetraacetic acid (sodium EDTA). It can cause irritation to the skin, eyes, and respiratory system.

Opening Strategy

Demonstrate the cleaning abilities of soap by having some students rub vegetable oil or shortening on their hands and then try to wash them with plain tap water. After their unsuccessful attempts, give them some liquid hand soap and tell them to try again. This time the oil will come off.

Ask students if they can think of a reason why water alone does not clean hands even when they have not been coated with vegetable oil. (Natural oils produced by the skin trap dirt.) Ask the students if they think they could make a hand soap that is as good as or better than a commercial hand soap.

You may wish to remind students that both the liquid hand soap they will make and the commercial product they compare it with are actually detergents.

Procedure

Part 1: Making a Liquid Hand Soap

1. Use a graduated cylinder to pour 40 mL tap water into a 400-mL beaker or mixing bowl.

2. Add 16 drops of glycerol dropwise using a plastic transfer pipet or medicine dropper. Stir well to mix with a plastic spoon or stirring stick.

3. Add 0.3 g citric acid and 0.2 g tetrasodium ethylenediaminetetraacetic acid (EDTA) to the mixture, and stir until they are dissolved.

4. Stir in 50.0 g ammonium lauryl sulfate and mix thoroughly.

5. Pour in 2.0 mL lauramide diethylamine (DEA) and stir until the mixture becomes uniform.

6. Pour in 4.8 mL sodium lauryl sulfate and stir the mixture thoroughly.

7. Pour an equal amount of the mixture into each of the pump bottles.

Part 2: Testing Your Soap
A. Grease-Cutting Ability
1. Fill two jars about half-full of tap water. Label the jars "homemade liquid hand soap" and "commercial liquid hand soap."

2. Using a disposable plastic pipet or medicine dropper, add 20 drops of vegetable oil to the water in each of the two jars and place the lids on the jars.

3. Try to mix the water and oil by shaking each jar 25 times then allow the jars to sit undisturbed for 1 minute. Record any observations.

4. Add one pump-full of the homemade liquid hand soap to the oil/water mixture in the jar labeled "homemade liquid hand soap."

5. Replace the lid and shake it 25 times. Allow the jar to sit undisturbed for 1 minute. Record any observations.

6. Add one pump-full of the commercial liquid hand soap to the oil/water mixture in the jar labeled "commercial liquid hand soap."

7. Repeat Step 5 using the jar labeled "commercial liquid hand soap."

8. Rinse out the jars with tap water and use them for the Lathering Ability test.

B. Lathering Ability
1. Fill the three jars about half-full with tap water. Label the jars "soft water," "hard water," and "synthetic sea water."

➤ **If your tap water is not softened, you may find it useful to substitute distilled water for the tap water.**

2. Add 1 Tbsp calcium chloride ($CaCl_2$) to the jar labeled "hard water." Using a plastic spoon or stirring stick, mix the solution thoroughly until the calcium chloride is dissolved.

➤ **Hard water contains calcium ions (Ca^{2+}) and magnesium ions (Mg^{2+}). The 0.1 M calcium chloride ($CaCl_2$) solution simulates hard water for this test and contains a much larger concentration of calcium ions than typical natural samples of hard water.**

3. Add 1 Tbsp table salt (sodium chloride, NaCl) to the jar labeled "synthetic sea water." Using a plastic spoon or stirring stick, mix the solution until the salt is dissolved.

4. Add one pump-full of homemade liquid hand soap to each of the three jars.

5. Put the lids on and shake each jar 25 times.

6. Measure the height of the lather using a metric ruler and record the results.

7. Repeat Steps 1–6 for a commercial liquid hand soap and a commercial bar soap.

Extension

- Have the students calculate the cost of homemade liquid hand soap and compare it to the costs of several different brands of commercial liquid hand soap. Have the students graph their results.

Discussion

- Compare the results of the grease-cutting ability test for the homemade hand soap and the commercial hand soap.

- Discuss the differences in the height of the lather in the three test solutions.
  Because the liquid soaps are not soaps at all but rather are detergents, they will not be affected by hard water as real soaps will. In hard water, the calcium and magnesium ions react with real soap to form a white precipitate or scum. The reaction causes a reduction in the amount of soap that remains dissolved in the water and available to lather.

Explanation

The liquid hand soap that was made in this activity is simply a mixture of various synthetic detergents, conditioners, colors, and fragrances. A detergent is a cleaning agent that works like a soap, but includes a sulfonate group or a sulfate group rather than a carboxylate group. (See the "Preparing and Testing Lard Soap" activity for a discussion of the chemistry of soaps.)

Since liquid hand soap is a mixture, its properties result from the properties of the individual components. This mixture contains two detergents, ammonium lauryl sulfate and sodium lauryl sulfate, which are both anionic surfactants (have negative charge groups within their structures). A surfactant, or "wetting agent," is a chemical that lowers the surface tension of water. This allows the water to wet the surface more easily. The structure of sodium lauryl sulfate is shown in Figure 1.

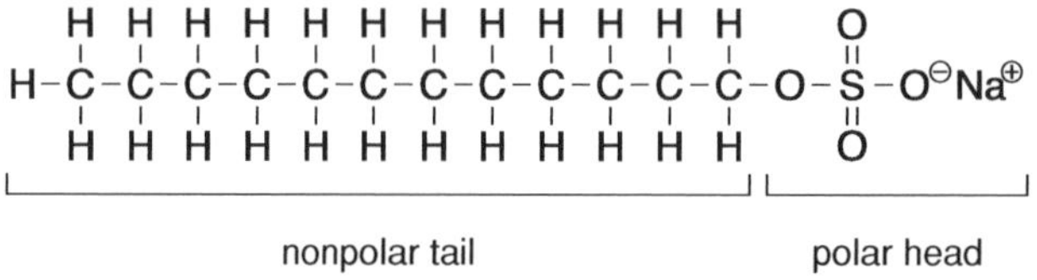

Figure 1: The structure of sodium lauryl sulfate

When placed in water, sodium lauryl sulfate dissolves to produce hydrated sodium ions and hydrated lauryl sulfate ions. The nonpolar tail of the lauryl sulfate ion is repelled by polar water molecules, while the negatively charged polar end of the lauryl sulfate ion is attracted to water. To escape from the water, the nonpolar tails of the detergent cluster together, forming a micelle. The amount or concentration of soap required for micelles to form is called the critical micelle concentration (cmc) and is usually quite small, typically around 0.01 molar.

When the detergent micelle encounters fats, oils, or grease, it absorbs the nonpolar material inside the micelle because of the "like dissolves like" attraction of the nonpolar species. Figure 2 shows the nonpolar part of the detergent ions and the fat molecules inside the micelle and the charged, polar end of the detergent ions exposed to the water. If large amounts of fats and oils are surrounded in this way, droplets of oil may remain suspended in solution and form visible suspensions. A suspension of a liquid in another liquid in which it is insoluble is called an emulsion. The detergent serves to promote the process of emulsification; it is an emulsifying agent. Through this process, detergents act to increase solubility. Surfactants draw the soil away from the surface to be cleaned and prevent redeposition of soil.

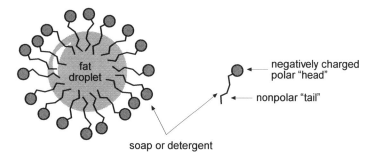

Figure 2: A cross-section of a simulated micelle

The main component in the liquid hand soap is water which serves as a diluent for the other components. The lauramide DEA acts as a thickener and a foam booster. Most people associate high lathering ability with excellent cleaning power. In actuality, lathering ability and cleaning power are not related. Some surfactants are low-foaming but will clean equally as well as high-foaming surfactants on a particular soil. Glycerol is added as a humectant to prevent the skin from drying out. The anhydrous citric acid adjusts the pH of the solution so that it is about the same as the pH of human skin, which is about 5.5. The tetrasodium EDTA (ethylenediaminetetraacetic acid) is used to complex with the ions in hard water such as calcium and magnesium, thus allowing the liquid hand soap to lather better. Table 1 lists the function of each of the components of the liquid hand soap mixture.

Table 1: Functions of Components in the Homemade Liquid Hand Soap

Component	Function
ammonium lauryl sulfate	detergent, foaming agent, and anionic surfactant
sodium lauryl sulfate	detergent, foaming agent, and anionic surfactant
water	diluent
lauramide DEA	thickener and foam booster
glycerol	humectant or conditioner
anhydrous citric acid	pH adjuster
tetrasodium EDTA	water softener

Key Science Concepts

- mixtures
- soaps and detergents

Cross-Curricular Integration

Language Arts

Have the students write commercials or slogans to market their hand soap and its properties.

Life Science

Discuss the use of soap in personal hygiene and disease prevention.

Mathematics

Calculate amounts of ingredients to be added if a larger or smaller batch should be made.

Social Studies

Have the students investigate the preparation of soap in different cultures or over different time periods in history.

Reference

Selinger, B. *Chemistry in the Marketplace,* 4th ed.; Harcourt, Brace, and Jovanovich: Sydney, Australia, 1989; pp 37–40.

Preparing and Testing Lard Soap

6

How did pioneers make soap for washing clothes and for bathing? Can we still make that soap today? What were some of the properties of that "lye" soap? This activity allows students to make lye soap from lard and test its properties versus a commercial brand bar soap.

Recommended Grade Level 7–12
Group Size .... 1–4 students
Time for Preparation .... 15–20 minutes
Time for Procedure .... 70–100 minutes (+ 60 minutes for salting out)

Materials

Procedure, Part 1
Per Group
- 10 g lard
- 15 g solid sodium hydroxide (NaOH)
- 50 g table salt (sodium chloride, NaCl)
- 20 mL rubbing alcohol (70% isopropyl alcohol solution)
- 250-mL and 400-mL beaker
- 100-mL graduated cylinder
- stirring rod
- small spoon or spatula
- watch glass for 250-mL beaker
- balance
- 1 of the following sources of heat:
  ○ hot plate (stirring model, if available)
  ○ Bunsen burner, ring stand, ring clamp, and wire gauze
- goggles

Procedure, Part 2
Per Group
- 3 small samples of the lard soap prepared in Part 1
- 3 small samples of a commercial bar soap
- 40 mL rubbing alcohol
- 40 mL of 0.1 M calcium chloride solution ($CaCl_2$) (See Getting Ready.)
- 5–10 drops 0.01 M sodium hydroxide solution (NaOH) (See Getting Ready.)
- 4 drops phenolphthalein indicator
- 2 100-mL graduated cylinders
- 4 10-cm x 10-cm (4-in x 4-in) squares of plastic wrap or aluminum foil
- 2 50-mL beakers
- hot plate
- masking tape and marker for labels
- (optional) stirring rod
- goggles

Per Class
- knife or hammer
- 1-L beaker

Resources

Sodium hydroxide, phenolphthalein, and calcium chloride can be purchased from chemical supply companies. (See Chemical Supply Companies at the end of this book.)

Lard, rubbing alcohol, table salt, plastic wrap, aluminum foil, and commercial bar soap can be purchased from pharmacies and grocery stores. Solid sodium hydroxide can be purchased as lye from grocery stores. Calcium chloride can be purchased as sidewalk deicer from grocery and hardware stores.

Safety and Disposal

Goggles should be worn when performing this activity. Dust, pellets, and solutions of sodium hydroxide (NaOH) are very caustic. Sodium hydroxide can cause severe chemical burns and destroy cell membranes. Contact with the skin and the eyes must be prevented. Should contact occur, rinse the affected area with water for 15 minutes. If the contact involves the eyes, medical attention should be sought while the rinsing is occurring. Eye protection is required because the heat given off in the dissolving process can cause splattering. Large quantities of heat are released during the dilution. Care should be taken when handling the hot beaker. The unused sodium hydroxide solution can be saved for future use or can be diluted with water and flushed down the drain.

Rubbing alcohol (70% isopropyl alcohol solution) is intended for external use only. Rubbing alcohol is flammable; keep away from flames.

The soap made in this activity is not meant for use in washing the body. Washing of the hands may be permitted with thorough rinsing. After the activity has been completed, any unwanted soap can be discarded in the trash.

Getting Ready

1. Prepare a 0.1 M calcium chloride solution ($CaCl_2$) by dissolving 1.7 g calcium chloride in 150 mL water.

2. Prepare a 0.01 M sodium hydroxide solution (NaOH) by dissolving 0.2 g sodium hydroxide pellets in 500 mL water.

3. For the testing done in Part 2, break the commercial bar soap into small pieces (about the size of a dime) using a knife or a hammer.

Opening Strategy

Discuss the procedure pioneers used to make soap. Fat drippings were collected in a kettle on the back of the stove. Hot water was poured through wood ashes to dissolve the potash (potassium carbonate, K_2CO_3) from the ashes. Next the fat and potash were boiled together.

The result was a harsh soap that was cut into bars for use in the home. This soap had a tendency to make hands rough and red because it was very difficult to add the correct amount of potash to react with the fat, and excess potash, which is a base, was left in the soap. Those who could afford it bought lye (NaOH) to use instead of potash, but the inability to measure out stoichiometric quantities remained a problem. Discuss uses for lard soap with the students. (Because of the effort required to make it and the safety risks involved, soap was a precious commodity on the American frontier and was used for cleaning clothes and cooking utensils instead of human bodies. Many fatalities and injuries of homemakers including blindness occurred during the soap-making process due to the corrosiveness of potash.)

Procedure

Part 1: Preparing Lard Soap

1. Place 50 g table salt (sodium chloride, NaCl) and 175 mL water in the 400-mL beaker and stir to dissolve.

2. Using a small spoon or spatula, place 15 g solid sodium hydroxide (NaOH) into a 250-mL beaker containing 10 g lard, 20 mL rubbing alcohol (70% isopropyl alcohol solution), and 20 mL water. Stir the mixture with a stirring rod.

Take care when heating the soap solution in the next step. While boiling, the solution could splash onto the skin. If contact occurs, immediately rinse the affected area with water for at least 15 minutes. See Safety and Disposal.

3. While stirring, heat the 250-mL beaker and its contents until it comes to a gentle boil. Continue heating and stirring until the lard dissolves. If necessary, add water to the beaker to keep the volume approximately constant.

4. When the contents of the 250-mL beaker have liquefied, pour the contents into the 400-mL beaker containing the salt solution made in Step 1. As the contents of the beaker cool, soap will form on the surface.

If soap has already started to form on top of the solution, you may need to use a stirring rod to pour off the solution.

5. After 1 hour (or overnight depending on the time constraints), pour off the liquid in the 400-mL beaker and rinse the remaining soap in approximately 200 mL tap water. The lard soap will be semi-solid.

Part 2: Comparing Soap Properties
Test A: Lathering Ability

1. Place a small sample (about the size of a dime) of the lard soap into a 100-mL graduated cylinder and label the cylinder "lard soap."

2. Repeat Step 1 for a sample of a commercial bar soap. Label the cylinder "bar soap."

3. Add 30 mL water to each cylinder and cover the top of the graduated cylinders with plastic wrap or aluminum foil.

4. Shake each cylinder 25 times and record the amount of lather formed by noting the volume marking to which the lather rises.

5. Discard the solutions down the drain and rinse the graduated cylinders for use in Test B.

Test B: Behavior in "Hard" Water

Hard water contains calcium ions (Ca^{2+}) and magnesium ions (Mg^{2+}). The 0.1 M calcium chloride (CaCl$_2$) solution simulates hard water for this test and contains a much larger concentration of calcium ions than typical natural samples of hard water.

1. Place soap samples in the graduated cylinders as in Test A, Steps 1–2.

2. Add 20 mL 0.1 M calcium chloride solution (CaCl$_2$) to each cylinder and cover the cylinders with plastic wrap or aluminum foil.

3. Shake each cylinder 25 times and record any observations.

4. Discard the solutions down the drain.

Test C: Excess Alkali

Do not use an open flame when heating the alcohol. Isopropyl alcohol is flammable.

1. Pour 20 mL rubbing alcohol (70% isopropyl alcohol) into a 50-mL beaker and, using a hot plate, heat it to a gentle boil.

2. Add 2 drops of phenolphthalein indicator to the hot rubbing alcohol solution and enough drops (very few) of 0.01 M sodium hydroxide solution (NaOH) to attain a very pale pink color.

3. Remove the beaker from the hot plate and stir in a small amount (about the size of a dime) of the lard soap. Return the beaker to the hot plate and resume heating until the alcohol solution boils gently.

4. Observe the color of the heated solution. Carefully remove the beaker from the hot plate and allow to cool. Record any observations.

5. Repeat Steps 1–4 for the commercial bar soap.

Discussion

- Discuss the lathering ability of the lard soap as compared to the commercial bar soap.
  The lard soap did not lather as much as the commercial bar soap.

- Discuss the behavior of the soaps in hard water.
  Hard water contains calcium and magnesium salts which react with soap to form the white precipitate we commonly call "scum."

- Discuss the results of the excess alkali test for the lard soap and the commercial bar soap.
  The lard soap contained excess alkali, a base, and turned the phenolphthalein/rubbing alcohol solution to a bright pink color. Commercial soaps are tested for this and have the excess base neutralized before the soap is packaged and sold.

Explanation

In the traditional way of making soap, animal fats were boiled in water with a base such as lye (sodium hydroxide, NaOH) which was purchased commercially or with potash (potassium carbonate, K$_2$CO$_3$) which was extracted from wood ashes with water. In the process, the triglycerides in the animal fats are first broken down to give long-chain fatty acids and glycerol (glycerin). (See Figure 1.) The fatty acids then react with the excess base that is present to form soap. Soaps are soluble salts of long-chain fatty acids.

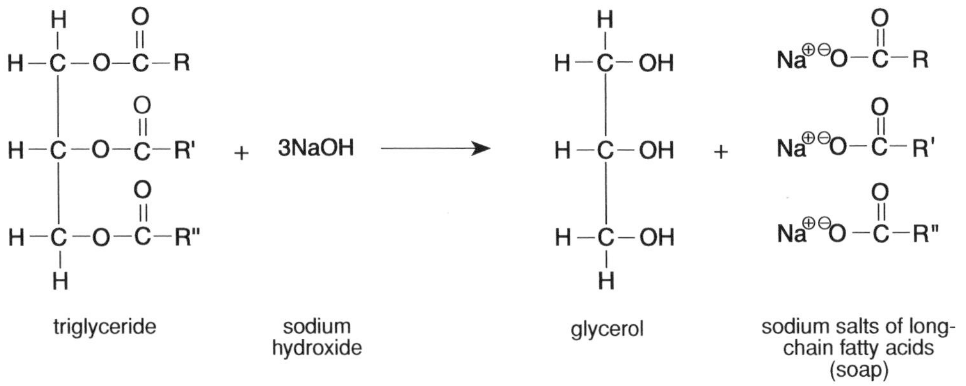

Figure 1: The traditional soap-making process
(R, R', and R" are the same or different long-chain hydrocarbon groups.)

The "salting out" technique uses table salt (sodium chloride, NaCl) to remove the soap from solution. Salting out is a special application of the common ion effect. The presence of the sodium ion (Na^+) decreases the solubility of the soap (which is a sodium salt of the fatty acids present in the lard) in the solution and makes it easier to remove. Consequently, these soaps contain a small amount of sodium chloride remaining from this process. Moreover, the glycerol produced from splitting of the triglycerides in the fat is left behind in the soap and in the water from the solution.

In this activity, rubbing alcohol (70% isopropyl alcohol solution) is included as an ingredient, although it is not part of the traditional soap-making recipe. By providing a medium in which both the triglycerides (from the lard) and the base are soluble, the isopropyl alcohol helps the soap-forming reaction to occur in a reasonable time period. This method also leaves the glycerol produced by the reaction in the soap.

In Part 2, the lathering ability, behavior in hard water, and presence of excess alkali are tested for lard soap and commercial soap. Lather consists of air bubbles trapped in solution by soap. The lard soap gives very little lather. Interestingly, although consumers feel that a high volume of lather means that the soap "works" better, the amount of lather has nothing to do with the ability of a soap to clean.

In hard water, lard soap forms a white precipitate which consists of the calcium salts (Ca^{2+}) of the fatty acids found in the soap. Calcium salts are much less soluble than the sodium salts (Na^+).

The test for excess alkalinity is done in commercial soap making. Because soaps are salts of weak acids (fatty acids), the pH of their solutions is not neutral (7), but rather basic (9.0-9.5). The pale pink color of the alcohol solution with phenolphthalein before the soap is added is indicative of a pH around 9.0–9.5. If the added soap contains unreacted strong base, the pH increases and the color becomes deeper red. If unreacted fatty acid is present, the pH decreases and the indicator becomes colorless. If beakers containing pale pink phenolphthalein are allowed to stand in the air as in the activity, the color disappears due to absorption of carbon dioxide gas (CO_2) from the air which produces carbonic acid.

Key Science Concepts

- acid/base indicators
- common ion effect
- soaps and their properties
- solubility

Cross-Curricular Integration

Life Science
Discuss the use of soap in personal hygiene and disease prevention.

Social Studies
Have the students research the preparation of soap in different cultures or over different times in history.

References

American Chemical Society, *ChemCom: Chemistry in the Community;* Kendall/Hunt: Dubuque, IA, 1988; pp 58–63, 426–429.

Bramson, A. *Soap: Making It, Enjoying It,* 2nd ed.; Workman: New York, 1975.

How Do We Clean Cold Surfaces?

Ever think about how freezers can be cleaned without having to warm them up? Would you use soap and water? If so, what problems might you encounter? In this activity, students face this challenge and explore possible substitutes for soap and water.

Recommended Grade Level 5–9
Group Size .... 1–4 students
Time for Preparation .... 25 minutes
Time for Procedure .... 25–35 minutes

Materials

Opening Strategy
- frozen ice pack or ice/salt bath (See Getting Ready.)
- disposable plastic pipet

Procedure
Per Group
- 6 8-oz paper cups
- 6 disposable plastic pipets or droppers
- cotton swabs
- plastic spoon or stirring stick
- ½ cup crushed ice
- 19 g (1 Tbsp) table salt (sodium chloride, NaCl)
- 1 Tbsp measuring spoon
- 8-oz plastic margarine tub or similar-sized container
- 2 pieces of heavy-duty aluminum foil, each 10 cm x 20 cm (4 in x 8 in)
- paper towels
- goggles

Per Class
- 60 mL (4 Tbsp) propylene glycol or ethylene glycol
- 60 mL (4 Tbsp) rubbing alcohol (70% isopropyl alcohol solution)
- 19 g (1 Tbsp) table salt
- 13 g (1 Tbsp) table sugar (sucrose)
- 7 mL (about ½ Tbsp) dishwashing liquid
- 1 Tbsp fine sand or dirt
- 100-mL graduated cylinder
- plastic spoon or stirring stick
- markers for labeling cups
- cups or other containers to accommodate the solutions prepared in Getting Ready
- access to a freezer
- (optional) food colors

Variation
- 5 5-oz paper cups
- 38 g (2 Tbsp) table salt
- plastic spoon or stirring stick

Resources

Propylene glycol, ethylene glycol, and disposable plastic pipets can be purchased from chemical supply companies. (See Chemical Supply Companies at the end of this book.)

Ethylene glycol can also be purchased as antifreeze from automotive and discount stores.

Safety and Disposal

Goggles should be worn when performing this activity.

Ethylene glycol, the major component of car antifreeze, is toxic if ingested. If possible, use propylene glycol instead of ethylene glycol. Make sure that students wash their hands thoroughly after the experiment.

Rubbing alcohol (70% isopropyl alcohol) is intended for external use only. All solutions used in the activity can be discarded by flushing down the drain with large amounts of water.

Getting Ready

1. Prepare the five solutions according to the following recipes:

    Alcohol solution: Mix 100 mL (about ⅜ cup) water and 60 mL (4 Tbsp) rubbing alcohol (70% isopropyl alcohol solution) in a cup. Stir well with a plastic spoon or stirring stick.

    Antifreeze solution: Mix 100 mL (about ⅜ cup) water and 60 mL (4 Tbsp) propylene glycol or ethylene glycol in a cup. Stir well with a plastic spoon or stirring stick.

    Salt solution: Mix 100 mL (about ⅜ cup) water and 19 g (1 Tbsp) table salt (sodium chloride, NaCl) in a cup. Stir well with a plastic spoon or stirring stick until all the salt is dissolved.

    Sugar solution: Mix 100 mL (about ⅜ cup) water and 13 g (1 Tbsp) table sugar (sucrose) in a cup. Stir well with a plastic spoon or stirring stick until all the sugar is dissolved.

    Soap solution: Mix 100 mL (about ⅜ cup) water and 7 mL (about ½ Tbsp) dishwashing liquid in a cup. Stir well with a plastic spoon or stirring stick.

2. (optional) Add a different food color to each solution to make observations easier.

3. Pour 10 mL of each prepared solution into labeled cups for each group. Also provide 10 mL water in a labeled cup for each group.

4. For Part 3, create a dirt solution by mixing 1 Tbsp fine sand or dirt with 100 mL water. Make the mock walk-in freezer dirt samples by placing 1-mL samples of the dirt solution in aluminum boats (See Procedure, Part 1, Step 4 and Figure 1) and freezing them ahead of time for each group.

5. Place an ice pack in the freezer the night before the experiment for use in the Opening Strategy. The temperature of the freezer must be at or below −10°C (14°F). As an alternative to the frozen ice pack, you can use an ice/salt bath prepared by placing ½ cup crushed ice and 1 Tbsp table salt (sodium chloride, NaCl) into an 8-oz margarine tub. Place an aluminum boat (See Procedure) on top of the ice/salt bath. The temperature of the ice/salt bath will be about −10°C (14°F).

Opening Strategy

Drop several drops of water on a frozen ice pack. Walk around the room and ask the students what happens to the water. *The water freezes.*

Explain that this is a problem when cleaning a car or house window in temperatures below the freezing point of water (0°C or 32°F). This is also a problem when cleaning walk-in freezers (the kind found in restaurants or meat lockers). Unlike our home freezers, these walk-in freezers are not turned off during cleaning.

Ask the students how many of them have seen someone squirt washer fluid on the windshield of a car on a really cold day. Ask them why it didn't freeze inside the reservoir or on the window. *There must be something in the washer fluid that keeps it from freezing.*

Tell your students that they are going to experiment to find out what kinds of substances they can add to water to keep it from freezing at 0°C or 32°F.

Procedure

Part 1: Preparing the Ice Bath and Aluminum Boat

1. Place ½ cup crushed ice and 60 mL (4 Tbsp) water into an 8-oz plastic margarine tub.

2. Sprinkle 19 g (1 Tbsp) table salt (sodium chloride, NaCl) over the ice. Stir well with a plastic spoon or stirring stick. Allow the ice/salt bath to sit undisturbed for 2–3 minutes.

3. Fold a 10-cm x 20-cm (4-in x 8-in) piece of aluminum foil in half to make a square.

4. Make the sides of the aluminum boat by folding up about ½ inch on each side of the aluminum foil square and then pinching the corners together. See Figure 1.

Figure 1: Making an aluminum foil boat

5. Stir the ice/salt bath with a stirring stick or plastic spoon. Place the aluminum boat on the ice/salt bath so that most of the surface of the boat is in contact with the ice. Proceed immediately to Part 2.

Part 2: To Freeze or Not to Freeze?

1. Obtain samples of water and the five solutions prepared in Getting Ready: antifreeze solution, alcohol solution, salt solution, sugar solution, and soap solution.

2. Predict whether each sample will freeze when placed in the aluminum boat on the ice/salt bath. Record your predictions.

3. Using a different disposable plastic pipet for each solution, place 1–2 drops of each solution and of the water in different places inside the aluminum boat. Place the drops far enough apart so that the solutions won't run together.

4. Record your observations after 3–5 minutes and compare them to your predictions.

Part 3: The Freezer Dilemma

1. Place one of the mock walk-in freezer dirt samples in its aluminum boat (prepared in Getting Ready) on the ice/salt bath.

2. Test one of the solutions that remained liquid (i.e., did not freeze) from Part 2 by trying to clean an area of the mock walk-in freezer dirt sample about 1.5 cm x 1.5 cm (½ in x ½ in) in size. Use a cotton swab dipped in a given solution and record the number of strokes it takes to clean the surface.

3. Repeat Step 2 using a different area of the freezer dirt sample for each solution from Part 2 that did not freeze.

4. Rank the solutions tested from most effective to least effective in cleaning the walk-in freezer surface.

Variation

- Have students add various quantities (e.g., 3 tsp, 4 tsp, 5 tsp) of table salt (sodium chloride, NaCl) to 125 mL (½ cup) of water in paper cups. Place the cups in the freezer overnight. The next day observe which solution(s) froze.

Discussion

- Discuss reasons why some of the solutions did not freeze during Part 2.
  The different solutions were mixtures of water and other solids and liquids. The presence of the other solids or liquids caused the freezing point to be lower than the temperature of the ice/salt bath.

- Discuss the effectiveness of the solutions tested in Part 3 on cleaning the mock walk-in freezer dirt sample.
  The antifreeze solution was the most effective in cleaning the sample followed by the alcohol solution and the salt solution, respectively. The antifreeze solution worked best because it was the most effective in melting the film of water surrounding the dirt in the sample. Once the water was melted, the dirt could easily be wiped away.

- Ask the students to list other examples of freezing point depression in their lives.
  Freezing point depression is used when salt is thrown on snow and ice to melt them, when antifreeze is added to the radiator of a car to prevent the cooling system from freezing during the winter, and when salt is added to ice when making ice cream.

Explanation

Pure water freezes at 0°C. Most walk-in freezers are kept below −5°C (23°F), so the ice/salt bath used in this activity was a good simulation of the temperatures found in a walk-in freezer. Of the five solutions and water tested in the activity only the antifreeze, alcohol, and salt solutions remained liquid in Part 2 even at the subzero temperature. The freezing point of each of these solutions is below 0°C. Solutions have a lower freezing point than the pure solvent from which they are made. This phenomenon is called freezing point depression. How much the freezing point is depressed depends on the amount of solute dissolved in the solution. The more solute added, the greater the freezing point depression. The cleaners used in subzero conditions are typically solutions which remain liquid even at these low temperatures.

Freezing point depression plays an important role in other parts of our life. Ethylene glycol and propylene glycol are used as antifreeze to prevent car radiators from freezing in subzero weather and are also sprayed on the wings of airplanes to deice them. The windshield wiper fluid used to clean the windshield of a car is a mixture of alcohol and water designed to keep the fluid from freezing when it comes in contact with the subzero windshield. Salt is spread on icy sidewalks and streets to melt the ice during the winter. Salt is also added to the ice surrounding a container of homemade ice cream. The salt/water saturated solution has a lower freezing point (about −10°C) than pure water (0°C). Using this mixture provides a lower temperature, which allows ice cream to freeze thoroughly.

Key Science Concepts

- freezing point
- freezing point depression
- solutions

Cross-Curricular Integration

Home, Safety, and Career
Discuss the reason for putting salt on the ice in an ice cream maker.

Life Science
Discuss why cells of certain microorganisms can withstand very low temperatures while other cells are damaged by these temperatures.

Reference

Hershberger, S., Miami University, Oxford, OH, personal communication.

Release Agents

What do bakers and road repair workers have in common? They both use release agents. Bakers use nonstick pans or grease and shortening, and road repair workers use nonstick coatings in the trucks. In this activity, students investigate several compounds to see how well they act as release agents.

> **Recommended Grade Level** **5–12**
> **Group Size** .... **1–4 students**
> **Time for Preparation** .... **20 minutes**
> **Time for Procedure** .... **45–60 minutes**

Materials

Opening Strategy
- tin of muffins baked in a greased tin
- tin of muffins baked in an ungreased tin
- dish

Procedure, Parts 1 and 2
Per Group
- 30-cm x 30-cm (12-in x 12-in) piece of heavy-duty aluminum foil
- cotton swabs
- 6 3-oz paper cups
- bar soap
- 2 mL (½ tsp) liquid floor wax (Do not use spray wax.)
- 1 tsp vegetable shortening or oil
- 1 tsp petroleum jelly
- 1 mL (¼ tsp) hair spray or styling gel
- permanent marker
- goggles

Procedure, Part 1
Per Group
- wax candle
- matches

Procedure, Part 2
Per Group
- 1 mL (¼ tsp) paint thinner or acetone
- 1 mL (¼ tsp) household ammonia

Procedure, Part 3
Per Group
- 4 candy molds

Per Class
- candy for candy molds (such as chocolate chips)
- Pam® cooking spray
- butter or vegetable shortening
- ¼ cup flour
- small saucepan
- hot plate or burner

Resources

Paint thinner and acetone can be purchased from hardware stores. Candy molds and acetone (in some fingernail polish removers) can be purchased from grocery and discount stores.

Safety and Disposal

Goggles should be worn when performing this activity. Household ammonia and its vapors can damage the eyes. It is recommended that contact lenses not be worn when working with ammonia, as gaseous vapors may condense on the contact lens and cause damage to the eye. Use ammonia only in a well-ventilated area. Should contact with the eyes occur, rinse the affected area with water for 15 minutes. Medical attention should be sought while the rinsing is occurring. Close the container when not in use.

Acetone is very flammable. Keep acetone away from flames and heat, which could cause it to ignite. Acetone vapors are irritating to the eyes and respiratory system, and the liquid is toxic if ingested. Use acetone only in well-ventilated areas. Used acetone can be rinsed down the drain with running water.

Paint thinner can damage the eyes and is irritating to the skin and mucous membranes. If contact is made with the skin, wash thoroughly with soap and water. Paint thinner is flammable; keep away from flames and heat.

Standard safety measures should be used when working with matches, open flames, and hot wax.

Dispose of any used paint thinner by pouring it into a shallow pan or dish and allowing it to sit in a hood or well-ventilated area to evaporate.

Getting Ready

Before beginning the activity, place small amounts of the floor wax, shortening, petroleum jelly, paint thinner, ammonia, and hairspray into labeled 3-oz paper cups for each group. Be sure to keep the containers of ammonia and paint thinner covered.

You may want begin heating the candy before the activity begins so that the candy will be melted and ready to pour when it is needed. Do not make the candy in the lab if it is to be consumed. If the candy is to be consumed, only non-lab glassware and equipment should be used.

Opening Strategy

Bring in two tins of muffins—one pan that has been greased and one that has not. Turn the muffins tins upside down over a dish to catch the muffins as they fall. The pan that has been greased should allow the muffins to fall out with no sticking; the pan that was not greased should not allow the muffins to fall out unless the muffins tear. Ask the students why some muffins fell out but others didn't. Ask the students why greasing the pan is important. Explain that the grease serves as a release agent so that the food will not stick to the pan. Release agents also make cleaning easier. Explain to students that they will be experimenting with different compounds to see if they are good release agents.

Challenge students to consider the application of release agents on asphalt trucks to keep tar from sticking to the sides and bottom of the truck bed. Release agents are also used on walls and bridges to make removing graffiti easier.

How are asphalt and tar kept from sticking to the truck that carries it to repair the roads? *Release agents.* If you have tried to remove tar from yourself or a car, you know that it is very difficult to remove. The simulation in Part 1 uses wax instead of tar to determine the best release agent for wax.

Have you ever seen graffiti written on bridges, on signs, or on the sides of buildings? Most of the time, the only way to remove the graffiti is to paint over it, but now special coatings have been developed that can be sprayed onto the sides of the buildings and bridges so the graffiti can be wiped away. The simulation in Part 2 uses permanent marker instead of paint to determine the best coating to make removing graffiti easier.

When cooking, heat causes foods to stick to the surface of metal pans. Cooking oil and grease are used to prevent foods such as eggs, cakes, muffins, and meats from sticking. Candy molds are used to illustrate this concept in Part 3.

Procedure

Part 1: Asphalt Truck Simulation

1. Fold the aluminum foil square into fourths horizontally and thirds vertically. (See Figure 1.)

Figure 1: Fold the aluminum foil as shown.

2. With a permanent marker, trace the fold lines to divide the foil into 12 sections. Label the top six squares as follows: "untreated," "soap," "floor wax," "shortening," "petroleum jelly," and "hairspray." Label the bottom six squares with the same titles as the top six. (See Figure 1.)

3. Using a cotton swab, apply the soap, floor wax, shortening, petroleum jelly, and hairspray to about a 3-cm x 3-cm (1-in x 1-in) area in the appropriate area of the top six sections. For the bar soap, wet a cotton swab with water, rub the wet swab over the surface of the soap, and apply it to the foil.

4. Light the candle and drop melted wax droplets onto each of the areas in the top six sections. (See Figure 2.)

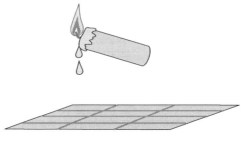

Figure 2: Drip wax from a candle.

5. Wait 10 seconds for the wax to harden. Using your fingernail or a scraping tool like a paper clip, try to remove the wax from the treated sections. Record how easily the wax was removed from each section by ranking the surfaces from easiest (1) to most difficult (6).

Part 2: Graffiti Prevention Simulation

1. Using the bottom six sections of the aluminum foil, repeat the application of the potential release agents.

2. Using a permanent marker, make three lines across each of the six sections as shown in Figure 3.

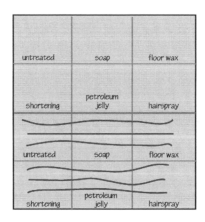

Figure 3: Make lines across the six sections as shown.

3. Using a cotton swab dipped in water, try to remove the marker line or "graffiti" from the top line of each section. Record your results.

4. Using a cotton swab dipped in paint thinner or acetone, try to remove the graffiti from the second line of each section. Record your results.

5. Using a cotton swab dipped in household ammonia, try to remove the graffiti from the bottom lines. Record your results.

 Observe proper safety precautions when handling or diluting ammonia solutions. See Safety and Disposal.

6. Rank the surfaces from easiest (1) to most difficult (6) for removing the marker line with the water, the paint thinner or acetone, and the ammonia.

Part 3: Candy Molds

 If students are to eat the candy, make sure that all chemicals and materials from Parts 1 and 2 have been removed from the area. Do not use any glassware or utensils from the lab for Part 3.

1. Apply a thin coating of butter or vegetable shortening to the first candy mold. Spray a thin coating of cooking spray on the second mold. Sprinkle a small amount of flour into the third mold. Leave the fourth mold untreated.

2. Pour the melted candy into the four molds.

3. Allow the candy to cool and harden.

4. Remove the candy from the molds. Record how well each release agent worked by ranking them from the best (1) release agent to the worst one (4).

Extension

- Do a cost analysis of the release agents used in Part 3 to find the least expensive agent.

Discussion

- Ask the students to report their rankings of the potential release agents for Parts 1, 2, and 3. If students' rankings differ, discuss possible causes for differences.

- Discuss the advantages of using release agents.
  They save time, they save money, they make cleanup easier, etc.

- Discuss how the use of release agents saves money.
  With the asphalt, road crews waste less asphalt because all of the asphalt is available to be used on the roads, not stuck to the truck, and workers spend less time cleaning out the truck at the end of the day. With the graffiti, the government and various companies spend less money on the release agents that coat their bridges, signs, and buildings than they would on repainting them. With food, bakers are able to sell all their goods and not have to throw away any cakes and muffins due to breaks and tears.

Explanation

Release agents prevent substances from sticking and make cleanup easier, thus making the appearance of manufactured products acceptable. Release agents do this by changing the properties of a surface.

Grease and shortening are commonly used in the kitchen as release agents to line the cake pan before the batter is added. This prevents the cake from sticking. Since the cake is easier to remove from the pan, release agents make cleanup quick and easy. Shortening is also used when frying foods to prevent them from sticking to the skillet.

Part 3 shows how butter and Pam are used as release agents for candy. This is similar to car manufacturers' use of release agents when making molded car bumpers. The mold must be treated so that the bumper is easily removed.

Parts 1 and 2 demonstrate additional applications for release agents. Materials scientists coat steel used in bridges, buildings, and signs with a release agent so spray paint used in graffiti will be easier to remove. This coating is made of a polyacrylate which dries, forming a clear coating. This coating is similar to hardwood floor finish. Before this coating was developed, removing the graffiti meant painting over it, which is very expensive. With the development of new release agents, graffiti can be wiped away.

Non-stick, silicone-based release agents are commonly used in bakeware. Similar coatings are also used on truck beds that carry asphalt to repair roads.

Key Science Concepts

- release agents
- solvents/solubility

Cross-Curricular Integration

Home, Safety, and Career
Discuss with the students the need for using shortening or cooking spray on the surface of baking pans or skillets. Also mention the non-stick coatings that are used on bakeware.

Why Should We Sanitize and Disinfect?

9

What does it mean to be clean? If a surface looks clean enough to eat food from it, is it really clean enough? How can you tell if cleaners are doing a good job of cleaning? In this activity, students test the effectiveness of household cleaners by determining how well they disinfect surfaces. Students will use agar plates to test control surfaces and surfaces that have been cleaned with various disinfectants.

Recommended Grade Level 3–12
Group Size .... 2–4 students
Time for Preparation .... 5–25 minutes
Time for Procedure .... 30 minutes (+ 5 minutes per day for 5 days to monitor the growing plates)

Materials

Opening Strategy
- shaving cream

Procedure
Per Group
- 4–6 of 1 of these growth media plates:
  - commercially prepared agar plates
  - plastic Petri dishes and raw potato or turnip, with knife for slicing vegetables and, if desired, rubber gloves
- grease pencils or water-soluble markers
- clear tape
- (optional) cotton swabs
- magnifying lens
- ruler calibrated in millimeters
- plastic bag and bleach solution for disposal of agar plates
- (optional) rubber gloves
- (optional) brown paper bag
- goggles

Per Class
- several brands of spray disinfectant cleaners
- paper towels

Resources

Commercially prepared agar plates under the name RODAC (an acronym for Replicate Organism Detection and Counting) can be purchased from Diversey Corporation, ATTN: Carol Marquardt, Cincinnati, OH; 513/554-4200; *http://www.duboischemical.com*.

Microbiology departments at colleges and universities or hospitals may make agar plates on a regular basis. You may wish to contact them for help.

Plastic Petri dishes can be purchased from chemical supply companies. (See Chemical Supply Companies at the end of this book.)

Safety and Disposal

Goggles should be worn when performing this activity.

If you are using commercial agar plates, time your order so that the plates are delivered no more than one week before you do the activity. Refrigerate the plates until they are used. Once the agar plates have been exposed to a surface and recovered, they should not be opened again. When the activity is over, put the plates into a plastic bag with a small amount of bleach solution. Tie up the bag and dispose of it in the trash. Treat the used agar plates as if they were rotten meat. Do not reuse plates.

If potato or turnip slices in plastic Petri dishes are used, the potato or turnip slices should be discarded in the trash. The plastic Petri dishes can be reused if they are sterilized either by heating in an autoclave or by washing in a bleach solution.

Getting Ready

If you are making the growing plates, slice the potatoes or turnips just before using. Do not peel the vegetables, and handle them only by the edges. The slices should be thick enough for students to handle (approximately ¼ in) and small enough to fit inside the Petri dish. You may want to wear rubber gloves while handling the potato or turnip slices to prevent contaminating the surface with germs from your fingers.

Opening Strategy

Discuss the relationship between microorganisms (viruses, bacteria, and fungi) and disease. Students may be surprised to find that the vast majority of these organisms are not dangerous to humans. In fact, bacteria and fungi are distinctly beneficial because they consume dead organic matter and recycle nutrients. Some of the bacteria that live in our intestines even produce important vitamins that we need to survive.

Ask students to name some diseases that are caused by different types of microorganisms. (Disease-causing microorganisms are often called "germs.") For example, the common cold and influenza (the "flu") are caused by viruses; pneumonia and food poisoning are caused by bacteria; and athlete's foot and ringworm are caused by a fungus.

Discuss the fact that microorganisms are all around us. One of the best ways to transmit germs is through direct contact, as with a handshake. This can be shown by doing the following demonstration with the class: Have the class form a circle around the room. Pick one student and place in his or her hand a large pile of shaving cream (this will represent a pile of germs). Have the "infected" student shake hands with his or her neighbor. Continue this until everyone in the class has been infected. Explain that since germs grow and multiply they are even easier to spread than was the shaving cream. Have students wash their hands. Discuss various ways of killing germs and preventing the spread of disease.

Procedure

1. Wash hands thoroughly with soap before beginning the experiment. If desired, put on rubber gloves.

2. Obtain two growing plates.
   ➤ **The first growing plate is to be used for sampling a chosen surface before any disinfectant is applied, and the second growing plate is used to sample the surface after it has been disinfected. Do not open the lid of the growing plate until you are ready to sample your chosen surface.**

3. Choose a disinfectant and a surface (e.g., a desktop, waste basket, restroom sink, cafeteria table, or any surface that can be sampled before and after being disinfected) to test.
   ➤ **You may want to have two groups do the same surface using different disinfectants for comparison.**

4. Sample the surface before disinfecting it. Rub a cotton swab across an area approximately 5 cm x 5 cm, take the lid off the growing plate, and gently rub the swab across the surface of the plate in a zigzag motion, or just place the agar surface directly on the test surface.

5. Put the lid back on the plate and tape it shut. Write the source of the sample and the treatment toward the bottom of the lid (e.g., "Desktop–not disinfected"). Also write the group number.
   ➤ **You may want to use a code for the source to save space. For example, you could use the number 1 to represent "Desktop–not disinfected" and number 2 to designate "Desktop–disinfected," in Step 7 below.**

6. Spray the 5-cm x 5-cm area of the surface with the disinfectant and wipe the area dry with a paper towel.

7. Repeat Steps 4 and 5 for the disinfected area.

8. Store both growing plates in a warm, dry, dark place. If needed, the plates can be placed in a brown paper bag to provide darkness.

9. Obtain additional growing plates so that each member of the group has one.

10. Remove the rubber gloves, if worn, and press two unwashed fingerprints on the surface of the plate or kiss the surface.

11. Replace the lid, tape it shut, and label it with your initials. Place these plates with the other agar plates in a warm, dry, dark place.

12. Examine the plates every day for five days. Using a grease pencil or water-soluble marker, draw a circle around any bacterial growth that you can see using a magnifying lens. Measure the diameter of the circle and record these results. Use a different color marker each day and keep a key of the color used each day.

Discussion

- Discuss the effects the different brands of disinfectant had on the growth of microorganisms.

- Ask students why it is important not to use the same cup as someone who is sick or why it is important to wash your hands if you have been coughing.
  The cup used by the sick person has many germs on it from the sick person's mouth. Your hand also carries germs from coughing. If you drink after the person who was sick, or shake hands with the person who was coughing, you may pick up those germs and become sick yourself.

Explanation

Microorganisms are found all around us; most of them are harmless to humans. In fact, many of them are beneficial because they consume dead organic matter, thus helping to recycle nutrients. Some microorganisms do cause disease. These are usually collectively called "germs," or, in more scientific terms, pathogens.

The process of destroying germs is called disinfecting. Disinfectants, cleaners that kill germs, are used in many situations where contamination could be a problem, such as restaurants, hospitals, food-packing plants, etc.

Many germs are transmitted through the air and can be spread during sneezing, coughing, and hand-shaking. Germs can also be picked up from various surfaces. It is obvious how easily such germs can be spread throughout a whole room. This is also shown in the experiment when students place their fingerprints or lips on the surface of the growing plate. Any germs that were on the fingers or the lips will grow and multiply. This shows the students how important it is to wash their hands before they eat or after they go to the bathroom because the germs on their hands can be spread to their food or to other people.

The agar used in commercial plates is a gelatin made from seaweed. It is routinely used by microbiologists as a moist substrate for growing microorganisms. Various nutrients are commonly added to promote or control growth.

Key Science Concepts

- disinfectants
- germs/pathogens
- microorganisms

Cross-Curricular Integration

Home, Safety, and Career
Have a microbiologist speak to the class about his/her job.

Language Arts
Have the students read *War of the Worlds,* by H.G. Wells. In the story, the Martians who invaded the Earth were killed by bacteria and molds that are harmless to humans. Emphasize the importance of disinfection and sanitation not only to humans, but also to other species as well.

Life Science
Discuss the relationship of microorganism growth to the spread of infectious diseases.

Reference

Sarquis, M. "Effect of Chemical and Antibacterial Agents on Bacterial Growth," *Science is Fun! Student Program Handbook;* Terrific Science: Middletown, OH, 1994.

Addressing the National Standards

1 Creating a Window Cleaner Company

Activity: What makes a commercial window cleaner work so well? Is it possible to make a similar window cleaner in the classroom? Which is more economical, the homemade cleaner or the commercial brand? Why are most window cleaners blue? These questions and more may be raised and then answered when the following activity is performed in your classroom. This activity also introduces students to some key aspects of the retail world.

Science and Technology Standards:

- Abilities of Technological Design

  Students implement a proposed design when each group in the class follows a different recipe to make window cleaner.

  Students evaluate completed technological products. They develop a method for testing the effectiveness of their window cleaner against commercial brands.

  Students describe results from the product evaluation stage of the technological design process. They discuss the effectiveness of testing criteria for window cleaners.

Science as Inquiry Standards:

- Abilities Necessary to Do Scientific Inquiry

  Students use mathematics and graph the test data using a histogram or line graph.

Physical Science Standards:

- Properties and Changes of Properties in Matter, Grades 5–8

  Substances have different characteristic properties, including the ability to dissolve other substances. (Water dissolves water-soluble substances such as rubbing alcohol and ammonia, but water does not dissolve oil or grease.) When combined together to make a mixture, the resulting mixture has different properties depending on the amount of each substance included.

  Substances react chemically in characteristic ways with other substances to form new substances (compounds) with different characteristic properties. The ammonia in window cleaner reacts with triglycerides in grease, producing water-soluble products.

- Chemical Reactions, Grades 9–12

  Chemical reactions occur all around us, including in the cleaning process involving window cleaners. The ammonia in window cleaner reacts with triglycerides in grease, producing glycerol and water-soluble salts of fatty acids.

History and Nature of Science Standards:

- Science as a Human Endeavor

  Scientific enterprise is furthered by the contributions of individuals and teams from different fields, including science, technology, and business.

  Scientists are influenced by societal, cultural, and personal beliefs and ways of viewing the world. Cultural preferences determine what products scientists develop and the characteristics of the products.

2 *Changing the Properties of Soap*

Activity: Why do most facial soaps contain glycerol (glycerin)? How do additives affect a soap's properties? Can other chemicals be substituted for the glycerol and still result in a good soap? Students investigate how the properties of bar soap change when various household chemicals are added.

Science and Technology Standards:

* Abilities of Technological Design

  Students implement a proposed design. They measure and heat Ivory® bar soap, rubbing alcohol, glycerol, and water, and pour the mixture into a mold to make a bar of glycerol soap.

  Students evaluate completed technological products. They compare the appearance and feel of several soaps.

  Students describe results from the product evaluation stage of the technological design process.

Physical Science Standards:

* Properties and Changes of Properties in Matter, Grades 5–8

  Substances have different characteristic properties. The types of substances included in a mixture play an important role in determining the properties of the final mixture.

* Transfer of Energy, Grades 5–8

  Heat moves in predictable ways, flowing from warmer objects to cooler ones. While not the main point of this activity, students do witness the phenomenon when the grated bar soap melts from the heat of the burner or hot plate.

* Conservation of Energy and the Increase in Disorder, Grades 9–12

  Everything tends to become less organized and less orderly over time; the overall effect of all energy transfers is that the energy is spread out uniformly. An example of this phenomenon is the movement of heat from warmer to cooler objects, such as the movement of heat from a burner to a pan to grated bar soap. While not the main point of the activity, this phenomenon is witnessed.

History and Nature of Science Standards:

* Science as a Human Endeavor, Grades 9–12

  Scientists are influenced by societal, cultural, and personal beliefs and ways of viewing the world. Cultural preferences determine what products scientists develop and the characteristics of the products.

Science in Personal and Social Perspectives Standards:

* Personal and Community Health, Grades 9–12

  Some diseases and illnesses can be prevented by good personal hygiene, such as handwashing with soap.

3 Lip Balm

Activity: What chemicals are used to make lip balm? How is it made? In this activity, students make their own lip balm and may be surprised to find that the product they make works just as well as most commercial ones.

Science and Technology Standards:

- Abilities of Technological Design

  Students implement a proposed design, making their own lip balm by measuring and mixing waxes, oils, and creams.

  Students evaluate completed technological products by comparing their homemade lip balm with commercial lip balm, using their senses of touch, smell, and sight, and suggesting improvements to the lip balm recipe.

  In an extension, students may design a product in creating their own recipe for a lip balm, taking into account costs, packaging, and product names.

Physical Science Standards:

- Properties and Changes of Properties in Matter, Grades 5–8

  Substances have different characteristic properties. The types of substances included in a mixture play an important role in determining the properties of the final mixture.

- Transfer of Energy, Grades 5–8

  Heat moves in predictable ways, flowing from warmer objects to cooler ones. While not the main point of this activity, students do witness the phenomenon when the wax melts from the heat of the hot plate.

- Structure and Properties of Matter, Grades 9–12

  A compound is formed when two or more kinds of atoms or ions bind together chemically. However, compounding, as used by the cosmetics industry, involves the mixing of two or more substances to obtain a finished product that is a mixture rather than a compound of a chemical reaction.

- Conservation of Energy and the Increase in Disorder, Grades 9–12

  Everything tends to become less organized and less orderly over time; the overall effect of all energy transfers is that the energy is spread out uniformly. An example of this phenomenon is the movement of heat from warmer to cooler objects, such as the movement of heat from a burner to a pan to a block of paraffin. While not the main point of the activity, this phenomenon is witnessed.

History and Nature of Science Standards:

- Science as a Human Endeavor, Grades 9–12

  Scientists are influenced by societal, cultural, and personal beliefs and ways of viewing the world. Cultural preferences determine what products scientists develop and the characteristics of the products.

4   *Making an Ester*

Manufacturers often add pleasant scents to cleaning products to make them more appealing to consumers. Many natural and artificial scents belong to a class of compounds called esters. Esters are produced by a chemical process called esterification, and in this activity, students will observe as the instructor prepares several synthetic scents that are esters. Students will have the opportunity to smell the esters that are produced.

Science and Technology Standards:

- Understandings About Science and Technology, Grades 9–12

  Science offers advances with the introduction of new technologies. Dowex resin, a product recently developed with new technology, is a less dangerous substitute for concentrated sulfuric acid. Either substance can be used as a catalyst in this activity.

Science as Inquiry Standards:

- Abilities Necessary to Do Scientific Inquiry

  Students explain how Dowex resin or the sulfuric acid functions as a catalyst in the reactions.

Physical Science Standards:

- Properties and Changes of Properties in Matter, Grades 5–8

  Substances react chemically in characteristic ways with other substances to form new substances with different characteristic properties; through esterification reactions, different organic acids react with given alcohols to form esters that have distinctly different odors.

- Chemical Reactions, Grades 9–12

  Chemical reactions occur all around us. In this demonstration, an organic acid reacts with an alcohol to form an ester and water. This type of reaction is called esterification.

  Catalysts accelerate chemical reactions. Dowex beads or concentrated sulfuric acid serves as a catalyst in this investigation, scavenging the water produced by the esterification reaction and driving the reaction towards producing an ester.

History and Nature of Science Standards:

- Science as a Human Endeavor, Grades 9–12

  Scientists are influenced by societal, cultural, and personal beliefs and ways of viewing the world. Cultural preferences determine what products scientists develop and the characteristics of the products.

5   *Making a Liquid Hand Soap*

Activity: Most liquid hand soaps are actually detergents. In this activity, students make a liquid hand soap similar to commercial liquid hand soaps and compare the properties of the homemade hand soap to those of a commercial brand.

Science and Technology Standards:

- Abilities of Technological Design

  Students implement a proposed design, measuring and mixing ingredients to make a liquid hand soap.

  Students evaluate completed technological designs or products with several tests. They compare the grease-cutting ability of homemade and commercial hand soaps by shaking water, oil, and liquid soap in a jar; they compare the soaps for lathering ability in hard, soft, and salt water.

Students describe results from the product evaluation stage of the technological design process.

Physical Science Standards:

- Properties and Changes of Properties in Matter, Grades 5–8

  Substances have different characteristic properties. The types of substances included in a mixture play an important role in determining the properties of the final mixture.

  A characteristic property of soaps and detergents is they act as surfactants (chemicals that decrease surface tension) and they promote emulsification of oil and grease.

- Motions and Forces, Grades 9–12

  The electric force is a universal force that exists between any two charged objects. The nonpolar tail of the lauryl sulfate ion is repelled by polar water molecules, while the negatively charged polar end of the lauryl sulfate ion is attracted to water.

History and Nature of Science Standards:

- Science as a Human Endeavor, Grades 9–12

  Scientists are influenced by societal, cultural, and personal beliefs and ways of viewing the world. Cultural preferences determine what products scientists develop and the characteristics of the products.

Science in Personal and Social Perspectives Standards:

- Personal and Community Health, Grades 9–12

  Some diseases and illnesses can be prevented by good personal hygiene such as handwashing with soap.

6 *Preparing and Testing Lard Soap*

Activity: How did pioneers make soap for washing clothes and bathing? Can we still make that soap today? What were some of the properties of "lye" soap? This activity allows students to make lye soap from lard and test its properties against a commercial brand bar soap.

Science and Technology Standards:

- Abilities of Technological Design

  Students implement a proposed design, measuring and heating ingredients to make lard soap.

  Students evaluate completed technological products. They test and compare the behavior of lard soap and commercial soap in hard water.

  Students describe results from the product evaluation stage of the technological design process. They discuss results from their tests.

- Understandings About Science and Technology, Grades 5–8

  Science helps drive technology, as it provides principles for better technique. Students apply scientific knowledge to advance the technology of soap-making when they use a "salting-out" process to increase soap yield.

Physical Science Standards:

- Properties and Changes of Properties in Matter, Grades 5–8

  Substances react chemically in characteristic ways with other substances to form new substances with different characteristic properties. When sodium hydroxide reacts with a fatty acid, it produces soaps, which are salts of fatty acids, and glycerol.

A characteristic property of soap and detergents is they act as surfactants (chemicals that decrease surface tension) and they promote emulsification of oil and grease.

- Transfer of Energy, Grades 5–8

  Heat moves in predictable ways, flowing from warmer objects to cooler ones. While not the main point of this activity, students do witness the phenomenon when the lard melts from the heat of the burner or hot plate.

- Chemical Reactions, Grades 9–12

  Chemical reactions occur all around us, including in the preparation of soap which involves a triglyceride (lard, in this activity) reacting with a strong base (sodium hydroxide) to form the salt of the fatty acid (a soap) and glycerol.

  Rates of chemical reactions depend in part on temperature. The lard and sodium hydroxide are heated to speed the rate of reaction. Reaction rates can also be enhanced by using appropriate media for the reaction to occur in. (Rubbing alcohol provides such a medium to solubilize both the lard and the base.)

- Conservation of Energy and the Increase in Disorder, Grades 9–12

  Everything tends to become less organized and less orderly over time; the overall effect of all energy transfers is that the energy is spread out uniformly. An example of this phenomenon is the movement of heat from warmer to cooler objects, such as the movement of heat from a burner to a pan to a block of lard. While not the main point of the activity, this phenomenon is witnessed.

History and Nature of Science Standards:

- Science as a Human Endeavor, Grades 9–12

  Scientists are influenced by societal, cultural, and personal beliefs and ways of viewing the world. Cultural preferences determine what products scientists develop and the characteristics of the products.

- Historical Perspectives, Grades 9–12

  In history, diverse cultures have contributed scientific knowledge and technologic inventions. In this activity, students learn about how American pioneers made soap and students make a lard soap. In a cross-curricular activity, students research the preparation of soap in different cultures or over different times in history.

Science in Personal and Social Perspectives Standards:

- Personal and Community Health, Grades 9–12

  Some diseases and illnesses can be prevented by good personal hygiene such as handwashing with soap.

7 *How Do We Clean Cold Surfaces?*

Activity: How can freezers be cleaned without warming them up first? What problems might result from using soap and water? In this activity, students face this challenge and explore possible substitutes for soap and water when cleaning cold surfaces.

Science and Technology Standards:

- Abilities of Technological Design

  Students identify appropriate problems for technological design, identifying the need for a solution which is effective for cleaning frozen surfaces.

  Students evaluate several completed technological products, testing five solutions to determine if they freeze when applied to a very cold surface.

Students describe results from the product evaluation stage of the technological design process.

Science as Inquiry Standards:
- Abilities Necessary to Do Scientific Inquiry

  Students use evidence from the investigation to explain why some of the solutions did not freeze and to suggest other examples of freezing point depression.

Physical Science Standards:
- Properties and Changes of Properties in Matter, Grades 5–8

  A characteristic property of pure water is it freezes at $0°C$. However, if antifreeze, alcohol, or salt is added to water, the freezing point will drop to below $0°C$.

- Structure and Properties of Matter, Grades 9–12

  The physical properties of compounds reflect the nature of interactions among molecules. When a solute (such as salt) is added to a compound (such as water) to form a solution, the properties of that solution are different than the properties of the compound alone because the solute affects the interactions among the molecules. This phenomenon is known as the collegative properties of solutions.

History and Nature of Science Standards:
- Science as a Human Endeavor, Grades 9–12

  Scientists are influenced by societal, cultural, and personal beliefs and ways of viewing the world. Cultural preferences determine what products scientists develop and the characteristics of the products.

Science in Personal and Social Perspectives Standards:
- Personal and Community Health, Grades 9–12

  Some diseases and illnesses can be prevented by keeping surfaces (such as the shelves and floor of a walk-in freezer) clean.

8 *Release Agents*

Activity: What do bakers and road repair workers have in common? They both use release agents. Bakers use shortening or a nonstick coating on pans, and road repair workers use nonstick coatings in the trucks. In this activity, students investigate several compounds to determine how well they act as release agents.

Science and Technology Standards:
- Abilities of Technological Design

  Students identify appropriate problems for technological design.

  Students implement a proposed design, using models to simulate the inside of an asphalt truck and a sign with graffiti.

  Students evaluate completed technological designs.

Science as Inquiry Standards:
- Abilities Necessary to Do Scientific Inquiry

  Students conduct a scientific investigation to determine which compounds are the most effective release agents.

Physical Science Standards:

- Properties and Changes of Properties in Matter, Grades 5–8

  The characteristic property of release agents is that they prevent sticking by changing the properties of the surface to which they are applied.

- Structure and Properties of Matter, Grades 9–12

  The physical properties of compounds (including the release agents used in this activity) reflect the nature of the interaction among molecules. The selection and application of release agents depend on the intermolecular interactions between the release agent, the surface, and the substance one wishes to prevent from sticking.

  Oils are carbon-containing molecules which are not soluble in water and thus are useful as release agents.

History and Nature of Science Standards:

- Science as a Human Endeavor, Grades 9–12

  Scientists are influenced by societal, cultural, and personal beliefs and ways of viewing the world. Cultural preferences determine what products scientists develop and the characteristics of the products.

9 Why Should We Sanitize and Disinfect?

Activity: What does it mean to be clean? If a surface looks clean enough to eat food from it, is it really clean enough? How can you tell if cleaning products are doing a good job of cleaning? In this activity, students test the effectiveness of household cleaners by determining how well they disinfect surfaces. Students use agar plates to test control surfaces and surfaces that have been cleaned with various disinfectants.

Science and Technology Standards:

- Understandings About Science and Technology

  Technology is essential to science because it provides instruments and techniques that enable scientists to make observations of objects and phenomena that are otherwise unobservable. In this activity, students test how well various disinfectants eliminate microorganisms by growing microorganisms on RODAC agar plates.

Science as Inquiry Standards:

- Abilities Necessary to Do Scientific Inquiry

  Students conduct an investigation by testing the effect of disinfectant on the growth of microorganisms.

  Students use evidence from that investigation to propose explanations for why they should wash their hands when they have been coughing.

Life Science Standards:

- Structure and Function in Living Systems, Grades 5–8

  Disease is a breakdown in structure or function of an organism. One way to minimize disease is to sanitize and disinfect.

- The Interdependence of Organisms, Grades 9–12

  Organisms both cooperate and compete in ecosystems. Humans use disinfectants to compete with pathogenic microorganisms.

History and Nature of Science Standards:

- Science as a Human Endeavor, Grades 9–12

  Scientists are influenced by societal, cultural, and personal beliefs and ways of viewing the world. Cultural preferences determine what products scientists develop and the characteristics of the products.

Science in Personal and Social Perspectives Standards:

- Personal and Community Health, Grades 9–12

  Some diseases and illnesses can be prevented by good personal hygiene such as handwashing with soap.

Chemical Supply Companies

Arbor Scientific
Ann Arbor, MI
800/367-6695
http://www.arborsci.com

Fisher Scientific
Hanover Park, IL
800/766-7000
http://www.fisherscientific.com

Flinn Scientific
Batavia, IL
800/452-1261
http://www.flinnsci.com

Science Kit & Boreal Laboratories
Tonawanda, NY
800/828-7777
http://www.sciencekit.com

Sigma-Aldrich
St. Louis, MO
800/325-3010
http://www.sigmaaldrich.com